"What a beautiful book! So readable, themselves. *Ragged Hope* is filled wi who are weary, worn, and wounded. that—hope that God can do a mighty work even with those of who carry the ugliest of scars."
—Debbie Macomber, #1 N

"If you have ever had to pi one else dumped a proble *Hope* will tug at your hea commitment to do the ne book! It is filled with poi that will challenge you to form upon which you can —Carol Kent, speaker and

" 'Survivors . . . don't inventory what they've lost but what they have at their disposal.' That's only one of the many insightful gems that fill this well-written book. With compassion and warmth, Cynthia Ruchti writes about people who made unwise, immature, or calculated bad decisions that threw themselves and others into chaos. And yet, even in the worst moments, some held on to what she calls rugged or true hope. 'True hope is indestructible.' Those four words sum up the positive message of this book."
—Cecil Murphey, bestselling author of more than 135 books, including *Making Sense When Life Doesn't*, *Gifted Hands* (with Dr. Ben Carson), and *90 Minutes in Heaven* (with Don Piper)

"*Ragged Hope* celebrates God's fingerprints in difficult, harrowing stories, reminding us that He can heal the deepest of wounds. Threaded with authenticity and real-life heartache, Cynthia Ruchti offers us all a pathway through relational pain."
—Mary DeMuth, speaker and author of *The Wall Around Your Heart*

"In *Ragged Hope*, Cynthia Ruchti meets readers in their unwelcome circumstances and opens the window to delightful rays of unexpected, God-shaped hope. Sometimes with humor but always with artistry, gentleness, and grace, she refreshes the weary soul through wonderfully crafted stories of real people like us. This book will turn you into a carrier of hope!"
—Jan Kern, author of *Scars That Wound, Scars That Heal* and founder of Voice of Courage

"This not a book for your shelf but a tool that must be placed in the hands of people who live in a culture where hope is often deferred, but the reality is that hope is knocking at the door."
—Jason Hirsch, Lead Pastor of North Ridge Church and Leadership Trainer & Conference speaker for www.IEQUIP.org

"This book is, at its heart, a celebration of human resilience and God's unfailing love and power at work to redeem, reclaim, and restore, as God shines indestructible hope into the darkest corners of our experience."
—Mary Pierce, professional counselor, speaker, and author of *When Did My Life Become a Game of Twister?* and other books of inspiration for women

"Read this book to find the strong hope that sings through the pain. Read this book to hear the truth that we are never abandoned, that God's steadfast love and mercy is bigger than anyone else's 'bad' toward us. Read this book for the questions at the ends of the chapters, as they help hope move into your heart. As a Christian psychologist and professor, I recommend this book highly. It packs a powerful message for all of us who need healing from life's hurts and who want to be pointed to hope's doorway."
—Betsy A. Barber, PsyD, Assc. Director, Institute for Spiritual Formation, Talbot School of Theology; Director, Center for Spiritual Renewal, Biola University

"As a survivor of more than one of the events described in this amazing book, I can attest to Cynthia Ruchti's gentle hand and powerful teaching on these tough topics. Anyone in need of a jolt of Jesus' power need only open the cover of this book!"
—Kathleen Y'Barbo, author of The Secret Lives of Will Tucker series

"How much will your choices cost me? Everyone has experienced the burn and turmoil of this question. *Ragged Hope* finely knits together the answer. The recognizable weak chords of humanity will draw you into each account, leaving you anxious to see where God shows up and how the balm of hope was applied."
—Angel Hirsch, minister to the broken, servant to the needy

SURVIVING THE FALLOUT *of*
OTHER PEOPLE'S CHOICES

Ragged Hope

CYNTHIA
RUCHTI

Abingdon Press
NASHVILLE

Library of Congress Cataloging-in-Publication Data

Ruchti, Cynthia.
  Ragged hope : surviving the fallout of other people's choices / Cynthia Ruchti.
    pages cm
  ISBN 978-1-4267-5117-2 (alk. paper)
  1. Forgiveness—Religious aspects—Christianity. 2. Conduct of life. 3. Human behavior. 4. Choice (Psychology) 5. Interpersonal relations. I. Title.
  BV4647.F55R83 2013
  248.8'6—dc23

                                                                    2013007962

These stories are real. In order to protect people's privacy, I have blended stories, changed names, and altered identifying details.

13 14 15 16 17 18 19 20 21 22—10 9 8 7 6 5 4 3 2 1

MANUFACTURED IN THE UNITED STATES OF AMERICA

To the wounded, the worn, the wondering.
And to those who let us
see their scars
so others can discover
Hope's hideout.

Contents

CONTENTS

Introduction

RON AND JUDY CALLED RON'S BROTHER AND HIS wife to say they have to drop their plans to split the costs of a vacation cottage on the lake. Their grandchildren will be living with them for the next who knows how many years. Ron and Judy's daughter, a single parent, met someone on the Internet. He lives in Brazil. Children don't work into his life plan. So she left her kids with the grandparents to pursue the man with smoky eyes and a sultry accent.

———

Sarah changed her locks. Changed her name. Eventually changed her address. He still found her. Stalkers don't obey restraining orders. Why did she have to leave a job she loved because of his sickness? Why is she paying the price for *his* warped thinking?

———

Dan sold his Motocross bike to pay for his artificial leg. The accident that took his limb—and now his bike—happened in a parking lot, of all things. Who drives drunk in a parking lot? Whatever his name was, he got away with it without a scratch or a fine or a jail term. He'd fled the scene and had never been caught. Dan now walks with a limp, emotionally as well as physically. Someone else's choice affects every day of his life.

———

I crossed the campus of a private college a few months ago while attending a conference. The summer work crew slipped into their tasks in sync with the exit of the past semester's students. I watched, fascinated, as two young men scraped old gum from the brick walkway between the grand, hundred-year-old buildings. The youth worked, bent and bored, with putty knives and sunburns. Scraping, scraping, scraping nickel-sized, tarry refuse from life's path. An hour later the young men had cleared only a dozen of the thousands of bricks the summer promised them.

Waste cans sat proud, ready, and unused a few feet away. Unthinking, a semester's worth of students had tossed their exhausted gum on the bricks. Now, men with putty knives spent their days mindlessly engaged in the tedium of cleanup.

Other people's choices aren't always life-changing. Sometimes they're merely annoying, mildly disturbing. We still need grace to cope with their negative effects on us.

The math teacher grades on a twisted curve, which adversely affects your grade point average, which means the scholarship goes to another student. Without the scholarship, your choices narrow. Now your workday looks nothing like you envisioned it. Combined with other factors, a teacher's decision changes the course you'd mapped out.

The upstairs tenants buy a dog—120 pounds of fur with bear claws for paws and a bad case of insomnia. The hardwood floor and lack of insulation between their apartment and yours accentuate the beast's heavy-footed tick-tick-tick, tick-tick-tick-tick from midnight to dawn. The dog's seeing a counselor for his sleeplessness. You wonder if the counselor takes people, too.

Your mother wears army boots. And a lime green tutu over her leopard leotards. She's not motivated by dementia, but thrives on the attention she gets at the senior center, on the street, at Walmart, and at church. Her choice of a comic life undercuts your longing for respect in the community. She's adorable. You're irritable. Everyone thinks you're the one with the problem.

Your friend inadvertently copies you on an e-mail intended for someone else. The message mocks and belittles you. Years of trust and companionship disappear. Delete is not a strong enough response.

Careless or cruel, thoughtless or depraved, the choices others make affect us. Short-term. Long-term. Sometimes causing indigestion. Sometimes leaving scars.

We labor to breathe through the fallout of what those choices mean to us, our sanity, our stability, our sense of well-being.

When we stand in a muddle of misery someone else created for us, too weary to be creative, too worn down to embrace a trendy problem-solving technique or follow a seven-step plan to a new, improved life, we need an arm around our shoulder assuring us God hears, God understands, and God is not stingy with hope.

How ragged is the hope you're clutching? It's no less valuable or essential than it was when it was new.

Is it hard for you to admit you're struggling with the aftermath of other people's choices? Did you think confessing how awful it is would make it worse? Or make your pain seem pathetic, or cheapen the tenacity you're working so hard to maintain?

Do the people you love and influence need a reminder of this timeless truth? "No one can measure the depth of [God's] understanding" (Isaiah 40:28 NLT).

Or are you the one whose choices have changed someone else's life and you too struggle to find a reason to—or a way to—keep hope from disintegrating to powder in your hands?

In these pages, you may discover hope, as I did, carried on the wild flood of *starting-over* words, *do-over* words, the "re-" words: restructure, re-create, revise, rewrite, refresh, rebound, reclaim, restore, resolve, reuse, relearn, recapture, relinquish, regroup, rebuild, rearrange, redeem.

Come a little closer. Tucked between the front and back covers are stories of people like you walking through the aftermath or the current hot zone of other people's choices.

Between the lines are the stories of those who caused the inexpressible hurt. As you accompany them all on their journeys, you may respond, "That's me!" or "Thank God that's not me!" or "I had no idea how far-reaching the fallout." Each story offers an opportunity for you to discover far more than insights about the reverberations of pain, more than a pinpoint of light for the path you walk.

You'll find hope that—even when it's tattered—glows in the dark.

1. Call to Arms

Lila

"THE LIGHT'S PERFECT IN THAT ROOM."

Don rubbed his wife's back. "I know."

"It's why we bought this house."

Don's sigh matched hers. "Or so we thought."

Lila pulled away from his touch, tender as it was. "I'm not trying to be selfish. Of course, we'll do whatever we have to. But I think I need a minute or two to mourn."

That's what Don loved about her. He could trust her to do the right thing, even if it meant sacrificing her dream of twenty-five years—a place and a time to pick up her paint-brushes again.

He was the one with tears in his eyes when they opened the door to her studio, the room that had so recently been cleared of clutter after their last child left the nest.

"We'll have to rip down my work counter," she said, "in order to fit bunk beds along that wall."

He nodded and made notes on a scrap of paper.

"And change the French doors onto the patio to a more secure window. I wouldn't feel comfortable with the grand-kids having such easy access to outside, or others having access to them."

Don read between her lines. Their daughter's probationary provisions allowed no contact between her and the children, but when had Meagan ever followed the rules? He made a note: *safety windows and a security system.* "That'll cost us."

Lila tilted her head to look at him. "It surprises you that Meagan's choices are costing us more than they already have?"

Don's "no" bounced off the untouched canvas on the untouched easel in the untouched corner of the fulfillment of his wife's dreams. They stood engrossed in the quiet that would soon end, a quiet they'd waited a long time to enjoy at this stage of life. A quiet they might not have for—he cal-culated the distance from the youngest grandchild to high school graduation—another sixteen years.

"Do you think she'll sign the papers?" Lila ran her hand along the shelf that held her color-coded baskets of art supplies.

"In a heartbeat."

"How could a mother surrender her children?" The last word caught in Lila's throat and came out half-formed. "That's not how we raised her, Don."

He addressed his scrap of paper again. "We'll need to call Jefferson Elementary and get the kids registered. And that means one of us will have to drive them every day."

"Car seats."

"What?"

"We'll need car seats for all of them."

Don looked up. "We'll need a bigger car, if we can afford it."

Lila pushed herself into his embrace. "First things first, love. You need a bigger piece of paper."

They stood that way, holding on to each other, as the perfect light disappeared behind the clouds.

"There's a positive side," Don whispered into her hair.

"The kids."

"We'll know they're safe. They'll know they're protected and provided for. They'll know someone loves them like they should be loved."

Lila put her hand over Don's heart. "They'll see what a real man is like."

"They'll eat well." Don rubbed his ample stomach.

Lila's smile broadened as if determined to lighten the moment. "Until we run out of grocery money."

"Do food pantries make allowances for people like us?"

"I guess we'll find out."

Groceries and car seats and bunk beds were minor list items compared to what Lila and Don would face in court battles and energy drains and shoulder-hunching concern for the motherless children.

The incidence of grandparents raising their grandchildren has risen profoundly, if what we see in our local community is reflective of what's happening in the nation. Parents in prison. Parents in rehab. Parents on parole.

Sounds like a preview of next season's reality shows, doesn't it?

Not all parents qualify to chaperone the class field trip. They can't pass the criminal background check or sex offender screening. What a world. What a world.

Many grandparents are left to pick up the pieces when the parent-child relationship is shattered by lousy choices, addictions, ugly circumstances, negligence, or—let's face it—stupidity.

The grandparents who handle it well embrace the children and the responsibility with grace. They adjust their schedules and modify their retirement plans—eliminating or postponing their dreams and inserting the needs of the children. They restructure their concept of "someday when . . ." They take a deep breath and plunge wholeheartedly into the commitment to raise another batch of children, though the responsibility belongs to someone else.

The cost can be astronomical. The payoff, remarkable.

Investing in the lives of children, investing in their emotional and spiritual health, their safety, their security is always worth it.

But between investment and reward lies a long stretch of expenditure and exhaustion for those tasked with the responsibility of caring for someone else's child.

"I don't want you to think it was all heartache," Lila told me recently. "We loved having our grandchildren around. We loved the input we had. The kids added so much joy to life." She paused. "But, it was hard. A hard decade."

She made the statement as if looking back on a difficult labor, with a bright-eyed newborn in her arms softening the sharp edges of memory.

I listened for a litany of complaints about what they'd been through, what Lila and her husband had sacrificed while they watched their grown daughter ping-pong through rehab centers, treatment facilities, and crashes. None came.

"Interesting way to describe what it must have been like caring for your grandchildren while their mom dried out. 'That was a hard decade.' So much lurks behind those five words." I watched as her face took on a serenity like the rich patina that distinguishes genuine art from a reprint.

Lila drew a hitched breath, then exhaled a decade of concern. "Now it seems it couldn't have been that long. But it was. I wonder if I slept a full night any of those ten years."

She didn't rush through her story. I didn't press. Some pain takes as long to express as it does to experience. I waited for Lila to set the pace.

As she gathered her thoughts from wherever they'd wandered, I considered how much it must have cost Lila and her husband to take on the obligations of the newest grandchild who came to them with womb-born addictions, with tremors and screams and brain cramps she inherited from her mother.

Unable or unwilling—*and did it really matter which?*— their daughter didn't set aside her drugs when she discovered she was pregnant. Meagan upped her intake to cope with morning sickness, her bulging belly, the clawing contractions that told her the alien she'd carried was about to explode out of her.

When Branilyn slid from her, screaming and trembling, Meagan's addiction told her she'd been freed from the pressure of a flesh-eating tumor. Lila and Don stepped in, paid for another round of rehab, and wrapped the unhappy child in their arms.

"Mom, you keep her," their daughter begged when sane enough to know what she'd done. "I'm no good for her."

No argument there.

Nursing Branilyn through infant detox and its residual effects while caring for the older children and emotionally nursing their daughter through her adult version of detox exacted a high toll.

"I want you to understand," Lila said, leaning in, "that it wasn't all negative. Hard, yes." Her gaze drifted to some year's ago soul-squeezing midnight. "But our grandchildren were a gift to us. Unlike many grandparents, we had the opportunity to influence their lives every day. We loved on them like no one else could, including their mother, at the time. We lived life over again through their young eyes and saw what we'd missed in parenting the first time around."

My mind rehearsed what it would be like to have a parenting do-over.

"They infused us with joy so intense it pulled a protective covering over the reasons they were with us rather than with their mom."

"You and your husband are remarkable people."

"Far from it." Lila's shoulders curled forward. "Giving them back to our daughter took more courage than we'd needed in ten years of caring for them."

"Your daughter's doing better though?"

The silence between us dripped with concern. Hope still had a fight on its hands.

Lila's smile recaptured the serenity I'd seen earlier. "Don and I are learning to relinquish the need to control the outcome. We can't fix anything. The best we can do is love them, make a difference where we can, and give God a wide berth to do what only God can do."

"You should write a book," I said.

"You are, so I don't have to. Remind your readers to watch for the glory moments when life gets ugly. They'll find them."

Watch for the glory moments? It's far more natural to watch for the *gory*, the awful, the misery-producing moments. "And here's another thing we've had to give up! Another hardship we shouldn't have to bear."

That approach may be natural, even expected. But it drives us deeper into the grip of the crisis rather than lifting us above it.

Artists through the centuries have used canvas and oils to capture a particularly poignant scene from the Bible. Jesus invited His friend Peter to get out of the boat and walk to Him on top of the water in the middle of a windswept lake. Peter obeyed. For a few steps, he rose above the natural pull of gravity and the laws of nature. Then he looked around at the waves and realized what he was doing was impossible. That's when he began to sink.

Love reached out and caught him before he gulped lake water. The artists' minds and ours wonder what would have happened if Peter hadn't looked down.

A friend of mine confessed she wasn't just conscious of the waves of her family's challenging circumstances; she was *counting* them. "Here comes another one. That makes eleven."

It wasn't until she got her eyes off the waves that she began to walk on top of them again.

Lila and Don could have drowned. They chose to look for the glory moments.

What if the prodigal son in the Bible had been a single parent? Who would have taken care of his kids while he rolled around in the pig slop of life? Grandma and Grandpa. They would have put a wing on the tent or outfitted the rooftop with bunk beds, walls, and a ceiling. They would have set more places at the table and then bought or borrowed a bigger table. They'd rock the children to sleep and try to keep their little ears from hearing all the gossip about their daddy's dumb decisions.

A grandchild in need is a grandparent's call to arms—both a call to action and a call to the arms of their embrace. No matter the cost.

And the costs demand more than one scrap of paper.

Reflections:

1. It isn't surprising Lila and Don agreed to raise their grandchildren. What's startling is the grace with which they did it. They resisted the idea of becoming martyrs in order to love and serve with grace. Does that make your heart clench? What sacrifices are you making for someone you love, but sensing the taint of victimization?

2. Don and Lila are letting life and God educate them in the concept of giving up the need to control the outcome of their situation. How strong is your determination to manage the results? When you think of the word *surrender* as it applies to allowing God wide berth to do what only God can do, does that introduce a sense of serenity or resistance?

3. Loving grandchildren comes easily. Caring for them takes uncommon strength and courage. If you're a primary caregiver for your grandchildren, what have you built into your schedule to care for your own needs, to refresh you and rebuild your mental and physical energies?

If you know a *Lila* . . .

Consider what it would mean to someone like Lila for you to be as persistent in loving her wayward daughter as she is. How much would it mean to the Lilas in this world if we stopped ragging about their children's sins and began treasuring the broken shards of pottery, the priceless though shattered people?

Do you know someone in the early days of a difficult assignment? Are you keeping your distance because you don't know what to say or do? Are you willing to ask God to reveal the role He'd like you to play, even if it costs you something?

*Let your servants' children live safe, [Lord];
let your servants' descendants live secure in your presence.*

PSALM 102:28

2. Spilling Coffee on Life's First Draft

Danielle

HE LEFT ON CHRISTMAS EVE. JOY TO THE WORLD.
Seventeen miserable years of marriage and he chose to
walk out on Christmas Eve and leave her with four kids, an
impossible mortgage, too much turkey for the holiday meal,
and a broken heart for her Christmas gift.

He could have left on December third. Or maybe
December twenty-ninth. Neither would have stung as much

as ripping such a joy-filled, holy night with such an unholy, gut-wrenching announcement: "I don't love you anymore. I'm not sure I ever did."

While others spent the holidays in Aruba or New York, at Grandma's, or at Aunt Marilyn's bed-and-breakfast, my friend Danielle spent the holidays curled like a dried carrot peel, muffling her sobs in her pillow, wondering how it could have come to that.

She'd found a marriage counselor they could afford. Her husband refused to go. She'd discovered a book that promised hope for relationships like theirs. He wouldn't read it. A marriage-in-crisis weekend retreat. Not on his life.

Those of us watching knew how toxic their relationship had become. We saw the disintegration. But none of us could have predicted he'd choose *that* day to move out. Even the completely heartless would either hang in there until the holidays were over or time their departure for a day with no family and holy significance.

In a twisted way, it fit his personality. Uncaring. Unfeeling. Unthinking.

I'm sure my friend wondered if she'd ever get over his abandonment. It's fifteen years later now. She's almost over it.

The consummate stay-at-home mom, she left much of what made her happy and dove back into the workforce in order to provide for her amputated family. The house she'd made into a haven became an albatross with faulty plumbing, too much lawn to mow, and leaky downspouts. She juggled exhaustion and her children's extracurricular activities. She explained until the words sounded rehearsed— *No, Jack doesn't live here anymore.*

When he filed for divorce, she dug deep into the couch cushions and borrowed from her parents for enough money to hire a lawyer. When she shopped for groceries after work, she bumped carts with the woman Jack chose over her.

"Pardon me."

"No, pardon me."

"Have a nice day."

Too many times, she apologized to little faces who asked why Daddy didn't show up for visitation.

Often when a man walks out, bitterness moves in to take his place. Danielle refused to let it.

She couldn't afford the upkeep.

That single decision, that counterpoint choice to his destructive decisions set their family on a path of healing. In divorce's game of chess, he checked by walking out. She checkmated by refusing to be bitter. Game over. Marriage dissolved. But she claimed an important victory.

Danielle's original design to create a warm, loving home for her children hadn't changed. She made revisions to her first draft and moved forward with those plans.

She refused to let exhaustion determine the tone in her home. *(Author's note to self: great idea.)*

Danielle prayed her way through her job and her single-parent duties. The distress that pressed her to cling to God for survival dovetailed with God's promise that He would in turn draw closer to her. "Come near to God, and he will come near to you," reads James 4:8. As Danielle tells it, God sat with her when loneliness hovered, coached her through decisions, embraced her when the wind howled and rattled the windows of her soul.

She refused to let her ex-husband's lousy choices dictate her health, her spiritual vitality, or her relationship with her children.

Was her future different than she'd hoped? Without question. Was it a future threaded with hope? Without question.

Not a neat and tidy hope, necessarily. Homespun, but elegant because of the mark of the Creator on it.

Her fists tightened around hope often in the early days of her crisis. Digging into its fabric reminded her that hope existed even when she doubted it would cover a scar that large.

Her husband was gone, but so was the toxicity in their home. The air cleared. She breathed in and out and kept moving forward.

Sometimes we find ourselves married to an idea of what we expect life to look like. You may have a dozen legitimate reasons to say, "This isn't it!"

If we hold that first draft too dear, it's impossible for us to move forward when the picture changes, when someone spills coffee on our only hard copy, when we realize the dimensions of our dreams don't fit into the realities of life.

"But I didn't want to be single/widowed/divorced/poor/ disadvantaged/physically challenged/alone."

Who would write a Version One with *grave disappointment* scribbled across it? We expect happy endings, expect the mysteries will resolve, the crises abate with us still intact. But other people make choices that mess with our happy endings and send us back to our expectations for a major rewrite.

Danielle rewrote her dream. A happy home no longer had a husband and father figure in it, but she determined happiness would still be in the picture. Joy didn't desert her on Christmas Eve; her husband did. His choice.

And her choice to live fully in spite of her pain, to find delight in those children in her care, to create that same warm, loving atmosphere she'd always longed for despite the drama of circumstances, meant their home—faulty plumbing and all—became and remains a haven.

Whose Christmas cards do I most look forward to receiving every year? Danielle's. Clever pictures of her kids and now her grandkids. An informative and stirring letter. Color and art and intense joy. Pictures of radiant smiles. Stories of fatherless but in no way loveless adventures building a legacy of memories.

The memory of that dark Christmas Eve is far overshadowed by Danielle's unwavering conviction that the date's truest meaning lies in the birth of God's Son, who came to bring hope even to a woman whose husband walks away on the holiest night of the year.

Understandable. That's what we would have said if Danielle's self-esteem had plummeted and stayed there. Her husband tossed their marriage aside as if it were a mustard-smudged fast-food wrapper. When the tears let up, anger was spent, despair was exhausted, disbelief was slapped into reality, and she regained her footing, Danielle walked out of the grief into an intentionality that provided her children with the security and stability they all needed.

She straightened her posture, lifted her chin, exhaled the stale air of what might have been, and drew in a fresh breath that filled her lungs in a way that made her think of God breathing into Adam's nostrils to give him life.

My husband's in the other room in his recliner. Faithful. Steady. Here. But that doesn't mean I can't learn something from Danielle's response to the consequences of her husband's choices. I want to be like her when I grow up. Resilient. Exhaling and inhaling in a beautiful pattern that enables her to breathe through pain.

Reflections:

1. Have you had to rewrite a dream? What elements of the new version have grown richer with age?

2. Is there a date that sickens you, an anniversary that shakes you because of the distress it represents? How would it change your attitude toward that day on the calendar if its dark memory were overshadowed by the imprint of a shadow-busting God, as it was for Danielle?
3. How can a person ensure that resentment and bitterness don't take up residence in the space left by someone's exit?

If you know a *Danielle* . . .

What can you do to soften the blow of the anniversary of your friend's darkest moment? Can you write a note or an e-mail that says, "I imagine this is a tough day for you. Please know I'm here"?

Can your family include Danielle and her children in an activity that will help create new, affirming memories?

What intentional thing have you done to remind you to pray for her?

I have loved you with a love that lasts forever.
And so with unfailing love I have drawn you to myself.
JEREMIAH 31:3

3. Scorched

Nora

WHEN I PULLED UP TO THE COUNTRY CHURCH TO speak for its spring banquet, I noticed two things. The mild weather had allowed farmers to get into their fields early. Tiny hairs of green feathered the neat fields. Endless rows of V-like tufts. Corn.

I noticed, too, that across the country road a house— a large two-story—was missing its roof and half its second floor. Charred timbers and hanging-chad drywall bits plus the whiff of acrid smoke told of a recent fire. Whose imagination doesn't kick in over a scene like that? I wondered what happened, how it happened, what was lost, and who survived.

"That was my son's place," a woman named Nora informed me when I'd finished speaking. "Across the road? My son and I own it. Four apartments, all rented out at the time. I know what you're thinking. No one was hurt."

I started to say, "I'm so sorry," but the thought was interrupted by her next revelation.

"Arsonist. They caught him. They caught the guy."

I suppose it doesn't matter how it happened. But the fact that it was an act of arson added another layer of ugly.

"That's a tragedy," I said.

"That's a senseless tragedy."

Gruesome words.

Four individuals or families suddenly homeless.

Mentally, I flipped through the detailed inventory work that follows a fire. *Oh, and a humidifier. We had a humidifier. And an electric grill. And Mom's . . . Mom's china. And my collection of . . .*

The broad smile on the face of the woman telling the background about the pile of ashes across the street startled me.

"We're rebuilding, of course. Better, this time. We're making it six apartments rather than four. Every one of them handicap accessible. None of us family members had a place where Dad would be comfortable, until now. We'll make him a great place over there. Close to church. He'll like that."

Would I have been thinking clearly enough to make plans so soon after the embers cooled? Positive plans?

Would I have had the courage to turn away from staring at the wreckage to focus on the future? How long would it have taken me to consider the possibilities of rebuilding to gain something not only tolerable but useful? Beautiful?

I wonder if all of the displaced families had the same attitude as Nora and her son. It seems rare. That's what makes rare things stand out—when they're laid against a dark backdrop.

As I write this, the trees outside the window are bent at the waist from a stiff, aggressive wind. I watch for one of them to topple. But they remain firmly rooted. They've been through this before. Their trunks sway, then rebound when the wind lets up.

A leaf just fell. And an old, dead branch. But tenacity keeps the trees upright. Whitecaps crinkle the water in the distance. Wisdom tethers the boats in the harbor on a wind-rushed evening like this. I'm safe in my borrowed writing retreat on the third floor—treetop level—listening to the noise of wind raking through leaves, the creak of tree trunks bent, then bending back.

A few weeks ago, a similar wind whipped flames that consumed someone's home and belongings. Wood and furniture were reduced to ashes, but hope wasn't singed. Hope isn't flammable.

Hope—true hope—is indestructible. It can be battered, but not extinguished.

That kind of hope endures through disappointment, delays, disruptions, and fire. Wishing is tinder-dry. The kind of hope God gives is flame-resistant. Nora demonstrated that truth by her inextinguishable hope despite the fire that claimed her son's income property and home and by her excitement about rebuilding.

Her reaction reminded me of the exiled children of Israel thrown into Nebuchadnezzar's furnace. They emerged untouched by the flames. The Bible tells us their garments didn't even smell of smoke.

If you've walked through the smoking-allowed section of a restaurant in days past on the way to the nonsmoking section, you know how remarkable that is.

How many weeks will it take for the insurance claims to be settled? How long will the cleanup take? Where will the residents stay while the new building is erected? How long before each resident realizes that one treasured, irreplaceable item is missing? Then what?

Long after the smell of smoke is gone from the property, long after the odor of new paint dissipates from the completed apartment complex, long after the arsonist is prosecuted, each one affected will remember the night of the fire. But I suspect Nora and those related to her will still be smiling. Not because life is easy. Not because it's "no big deal." But because they discovered the indestructibility of hope.

The arsonist stole a building but couldn't steal the family's tenacious joy. It remained unsinged. And that's what makes people like me say, "How remarkable!"

Before this book made it to print, the impact of this chapter sparked to life in a new way. My charred kitchen plunged me into the middle of the story. As of this writing, I'm a week and a half into fire remediation—onion rings gone awry. Flames of consequences licked the cabinets, the walls, what used to be my stove. Soot and extinguisher dust still show up in unexpected places . . . like the top of a box of cereal and the blades of the bedroom ceiling fans.

The house was spared. Gratitude is too pale a word, but I'm using it liberally anyway.

"A small flame can set a whole forest on fire," the Bible says in James 3:5. A small flame—consequences that stretch to the horizon.

Even though our fire was confined to the kitchen, an army of insurance people, fire remediation workers, and a battalion of details engaged in the blessed mess of restoration.

When I was the one pawing through the smoke in search of something to salvage, looking for the hope hidden under the twisted, toasted plastic that was once an under-mount light, I thought of Nora. She knew God promised beauty for ashes. So she went looking for it.

Those who look find.

Reflections:

1. How do you react to this statement? *Every time I see something beautiful and sigh with delight, I chalk up another defeat for the one who wanted to hurt me.*

2. As you sift through the ashes of how other people's choices—whether innocent, accidental, negligent, or arson-like—have significantly affected you, are you discovering unsinged treasures? What was left intact, untouched?

3. After a horrific tragedy like a house fire, survivors often report they shift their priorities. They cling harder to people and loosen their grip on things. They miss their collections but mourn lost moments. They slow down their efforts to do and ramp up their determination to be. What event or challenge if any prompted you to consider those kinds of rearranged priorities?

If you know a *Nora* . . .

Friends of ours lost their home to an electrical fire a few years ago. The community rallied, helping with cleanup, offering furniture, household goods, and a truckload of used clothing. Overcome with gratitude, the family was also overwhelmed with the task of sorting through the clothing to find the few items that matched their kids' sizes and tastes.

Time they could have used to focus on their plans to rebuild was spent hauling the excess to Goodwill.

Those of us closest to them observed the strain it caused, but no complaint passed the couple's lips.

If we want our donations to truly alleviate distress rather than add to it, we may have to get creative in the way we give to those in need and offer our help on their timetable not our own. My sensitivity in this area has plenty of room for growth. Yours?

When you walk through the fire,
you won't be scorched and flame won't burn you.
I am the LORD your God.

ISAIAH 43:2-3

4. The Swaddling Effect

Olivia

OLIVIA WIPED A DAMP SPOT ON HER FOREHEAD with the back of her hand, grabbed two oven mitts, and hoisted the pan of lasagna from its resting place on the kitchen island to rest on the trivet in the center of the table, not far from her equally spectacular salad and the basket of yeasty breadsticks. With half her brood of grown or nearly grown children already seated and eager to dive in, she playfully slapped at a hand reaching for a breadstick. "No. Not until we're all here."

The breadstick thief popped out of his chair and headed for the family room calling, "Come on, you guys. Time to eat."

They filed in, noisy and jostling, arguing politics and sports, elbowing for their favorite chairs while Mom made sure the oven was off and the cheesecake was where she'd left it—not guaranteed in a house full of food appreciators.

The ruckus quieted for a moment when she took her place at the table and surveyed the faces she'd loved before she ever saw them with her eyes. An empty chair caught her attention.

"Where's Tony?"

No one knew.

"Marcus, go find your brother. We'll wait."

Those last two words were met with expected groans. The lasagna gave off a garlicky steam that wrapped itself around the table and tantalized those already wielding forks and appetites.

"Marcus. Go find him."

He did.

Behind the garage.

Dead.

Family dinners will never be the same at Olivia's house. Nothing will be the same. Her son changed everything the day he took his life.

What could be more devastating than to lose a child? By his own hand?

And how could anything pierce more deeply than the grief that follows in its wake, tainting every family gathering? Every memory branded with the chronology—before his death/after his death. Future joy always smudged with guilt's rehearsals: "What could we have done? What didn't we say that would have made a difference? How could we have prevented this?"

Olivia later noted a kinship with King David from the Bible. He knew what it felt like to have a senseless act snatch a beloved son. Two, in fact. Second Samuel 18:33 says that "the king trembled. He went up to the room over the gate and cried. As he went, he said: 'Oh my son Absalom! Oh, my son! My son Absalom! If only I had died instead of you! Oh Absalom, my son! My son!'"

The expression of a parent's inconsolable broken heart— "Oh, my son! My son!"

Those of us not tortured by suicidal thoughts understand suicide solves nothing and creates inexpressible pain, a family fallout of incomprehensible sorrow. The victim's choice to end his life—whether recklessly or intentionally—forever alters the lives of those who care about him.

The circle of the hurting widens. Extended family, friends, coworkers, neighbors. *What could we have done? What could we have said? How did we not know how far he had fallen?*

The act of suicide is trailed by a wide wake of comforters. A flood of well-intentioned words. A memorial service grasping for hope.

Every heartbeat taps out a rhythm of grief. Each beat also

signals another moment having survived what was thought unsurvivable.

Within only days of finding his lifeless body absent his tattered spirit, Olivia's family reported hints of inexplicable peace lapping against the shore of their inexpressible pain. How is that possible?

How is it that children in refugee camps grab a scrap of a rag and knot it into a makeshift soccer ball? How can a refugee grandmother cheer them on as they play? Hungry and broken, they make a life in the camp that doesn't look anything like home.

In the face of their son's life-altering, agony-inducing choice, Olivia's family became voluntary refugees. They sought refuge in God's embrace, in the "protection of [God's] wings" (Psalm 17:8). They watched for and found evidence of the Father God's caring heart even as the ashes of the tragedy still sifted down around them. They found evidence . . . because they watched for it.

They're not pain-free. Far from it. Tears dot the tablecloth at every family dinner now.

But they have a Refuge.

It's not comfortable, but it's safe. It doesn't look like home used to, but love can survive there.

Faith isn't a sedative. It doesn't numb us to the realities of life's horrors. It doesn't evaporate the consequences or excuse us from the fallout. It is a refuge—God is a Refuge—where hope is shielded and kept alive against all odds.

Some—okay, many—of our questions don't have answers. Some of our distress has no cure this side of heaven. But we can draw comfort from the swaddling effect when God's embrace keeps us from running screaming into the night. He provides a safe place for pain's refugees.

Reflections:

1. The course of our lives, the path our heart takes, can change in an instant through our own decisions or those of others. When has that been most evident in your life?
2. How long did it take you to recognize that God stood waiting for you to run into His embrace?
3. Did obstacles stand between you and that Refuge? Pride? Fear? Doubt? How would you deal with those factors today?

If you know an *Olivia* . . .

What are the right things to say and do for parents whose child commits suicide? No one knows. You will show up when they need to be alone. You will leave them alone, assuming that's what they want, when they desperately need to talk. Or laugh. Or reminisce.

I sent a sympathy card to my friends. All it held was the assurance of my love and prayers and the watermark of my own tears.

We can improve the odds that our overtures will resonate, that our words will soothe rather than sting, if we make listening a higher priority than speaking.

A psychologist friend advises, "Ask what they prefer. 'I don't know what to say, but I want to be here with you, if that's okay.'"

Words are miserably inadequate at times. But a silent presence is simply eloquent.

Have mercy on me, God;
have mercy on me because I have taken refuge in you.
I take refuge in the shadow of your wings
until destruction passes by.

PSALM 57:1

5. House Hunting . . . and Hunting . . . and Hunting

Sonya

THE REAL ESTATE AGENT LOOKED UP FROM HER clipboard. "And your must-haves?"

"I'm not as particular as I once was," Sonya answered.

"Isn't it time for your dream house? At this stage of life, aren't you ready for me to find you everything on your wish list? Dream big. What would you like? Outdoor space? Four bedrooms? A master suite with a walk-in closet and *en suite* bath? Media room? Granite countertops? In-ground pool? Tell me when to stop."

Sonya let the shudder settle. "Stop any time. I can't afford—"

"You're not smiling. Let's have fun with this. When's the last time you purchased a home?"

"Twenty-two years ago. I thought it was the last move I'd ever have to make." Sonya pushed away the mental picture of the perennial garden that would soon belong to someone else, the pencil marks on the woodwork noting the growth of her children.

"And your budget? I assume you're single?"

"No. Married. Marty couldn't be with me today. My husband and I can't go over this price point." Sonya circled one of the price ranges on the form the agent presented.

The agent sat back against her burnt caramel office chair. "You're not making my job easy, but I'm confident I can find something for the two of you." She clicked a few links on her computer. "Here's a listing in Cedar Heights. Your children are grown and gone, I assume, but for resale value, it's a plus to have it within blocks of one of the highest-rated elementary schools in the state."

"No." The word came out like a sergeant's bark. Sonya closed her eyes. "Not that one."

"Okay, then." The agent didn't stifle her sigh. "This home just came on the market today. The second floor needs a little work. No problem for your husband, I'm sure. It has three bedrooms, a gas fireplace, recently remodeled and updated kitchen, open floor plan, right across the street from a beautifully appointed family park . . ."

"No."

"Something a little more cozy, then? Have you considered a townhouse? Semi-detached? You'll find the price on this one enticing. A mid-range townhouse. One shared wall. The young family next door travels a lot but even when home, the triple-thick shared wall means you'll hear virtually no noise from their children."

Sonya fumbled with the straps of her purse. "I'm not sure this will work at all. Maybe we won't find anything suitable."

The agent tapped a manicured nail on the desktop. "I never give up. We'll find something that appeals to your tastes. Tell me more about your likes and dislikes. Would you describe your interests as contemporary, mid-century modern, traditional, eclectic . . . ?"

"As I said, we're no longer as picky as we might once have been."

"A view? How important is a view?"

"Of what?"

"Water? The cityscape? A park? Golf course?"

"In *our* price range?"

The tap of the agent's fingernail revved up its staccato. "Let me take you to see the house in Cedar Heights. A quick walk-through. It will give us both a sense of what appeals to you and what doesn't."

"That's the one by the school?"

"One of the best in the state."

"Then there's no point in my looking at it."

Tap. Tap. Tap. Tap.

Sonya straightened her slumped shoulders. She couldn't bypass the dead-on truth. "We can't live close to a school. My husband's a registered sex offender."

The words vacuumed the air from the room, even as the accusation had vacuumed all the joy from Sonya's life three years prior.

She'd known something was wrong. Her husband retreated deeper into a cave of emotional distance, resisted attending church with her, needed something stronger than herbal tea to calm his nerves at the end of the day.

She'd guessed depression. Or burnout.

An affair? No. Not him.

She hadn't suspected the truth would come out when federal agents drew their guns, burst into Sonya's home, and confiscated her husband's computer equipment. Evidence. Evidence of the dark secret that changed their lives forever.

Plunged into an unthinkable world that sickened and appalled her, a world populated by disgusting perverts—and the man she married—Sonya fought for every breath, slashing at betrayal, self-blame, devastation, anger. The despair that engulfed her broken husband frightened her more than the fear he'd be incarcerated for his crimes.

He assumed she'd divorce him. What was left to love?

The shock that she stayed despite her repulsion about his choices helped restart his heart. She knew the worst about him and loved him anyway. It surprised even her.

Caught in a cosmic black hole void of answers, they spent the first dizzying days staring unblinking into an uncertain future and exposing all the ugly truth as if debriding a wound so it could begin to heal.

They prayed desperate, groaning prayers to the God whose middle name is Mercy. They told God their story when it was too soon, too raw to tell anyone else.

Catapulted into an unfamiliar truthfulness and transparency with one another, Marty told Sonya a voice inside his head blistered, "How dare you? How dare you presume upon God for help when your actions disgust Him?"

Faith whispered, "No pit too dark. No sin too wretched. He loves you anyway." They both heard it.

The list of consequences grew into a pandemic of prices to be paid. Every day it became clearer that the moral "gunshot residue" dirtied *his* hands, but the blood-spatter landed on *her*.

He'd lose his job as soon as charges were filed, and she'd have to keep hers forever.

He'd have to tell his friends, his pastor, his children. *Their* friends, *their* pastor, *their* children.

They'd have to move—someplace smaller, easier for Sonya to handle during his imprisonment, distant from playgrounds and schools when he was released. The lawyer they hired offered little hope of avoiding prison time. As the case progressed, the lawyer offered none.

Sonya knelt beside her husband when, utterly broken, he surrendered the last ragged tatters of himself to the Lord. She stood beside him when life or conscience forced him to tell the story to family and friends also affected. She held his hand when he retched and gagged over what he'd done. He held hers when she did the same.

Marty and Sonya found the first glimmers of hope through a faith-based freedom-from-sexual-addiction group. It told the raw truth, demanded honesty no matter how ugly, and laid out a healing plan that didn't settle for mere support. It held out for long-term victory. Marty poured himself into fighting for and winning his freedom from the addiction, though consequences and regrets lingered.

Sonya's normal reading list of classics and light novels changed to a list of disturbing statistics, legal recourse, and charming titles like *What to Do When Your Husband Commits a Federal Offense Too Revolting to Discuss in Public.*

Their extended families staggered under the news but remained upright. Propelled by an uncommon grace—*Isn't grace always uncommon?*—they chose to love even when they didn't understand how the man they thought they knew could harbor such a heinous secret.

The family chose to love . . . even when they didn't understand. They included him in family gatherings without prejudice and showed up for court dates. They silenced gossip without disguising the truth. They formed a tight net of dependable support that wasn't contingent on the outcome of the court's decisions.

Their church family—equally remarkable, a company of people healing from their own brokenness—did the same.

Leaning on those who walked beside them through the ash cloud, the couple retreated into God's Word, their only Hope.

A ragged piece of paper is tucked into Marty's Bible. It's a handwritten copy of the verse in which God says, "If you want to come back . . . you must really come back to me. You must get rid of your stinking sin paraphernalia and not wander away from me anymore. Then you can say words like, 'As God lives . . .' and have them mean something true and just and right. And the godless [around you] will get caught up in the blessing and find something in [you] to write home about" (Jeremiah 4:1-2 *THE MESSAGE*).

Sonya pushed through the stages of grief and watched in awe as God's tenacious love and hers drew her husband into a place of greater intimacy with God than he'd ever known. She'd seen fake humility before and recognized the genuine thing when she saw it in her husband's eyes. She witnessed healing in his heart and in their relationship before the indictment made it through the court system.

How did she manage? How does she today, on this side of the decision about his imprisonment, with the distress a constant companion and the consequences still as real and clumsy as a neon ankle bracelet?

She uncovered an answer to "What now?" when she read, "There is something I'm looking for: a person . . . reverently responsive to what I say" (Isaiah 66:2b *THE MESSAGE*).

Reverently responsive.

In the privacy of her imagination, she pictured Jesus sitting with her, sharing His own stories of a broken heart over the reprehensible ways His people disappointed and disgusted Him. He coached her through loving in spite of it all. He celebrated with her when there was something to celebrate and held her when there wasn't.

Sonya's decision in light of her husband's costly choices was to devote herself to growing in her responsiveness to God and reflecting God's extraordinary way of loving people when they're at their worst.

From their place of pain and humiliation, the two invested in preserving their marriage. Today, they're devoted to offering hope to others caught in destructive addictions and crippling remorse.

The wind shifts sometimes, dumping another cloud of ash over them. Remorse has a memory. So does the community.

As I prepared to take the platform to speak not long after hearing about Marty's sentencing, the worship lyrics projected onto the screen contained a major typo. And it appeared—same typo—more than once during the song. I know I wasn't the only one who felt the audience hesitate, then pick up the song again, recovering from the interruption and slipping back into an attitude of worship.

I used that moment to make a point during my talk. "How many noticed the typo in the worship lyrics?"

Many hands raised.

"Your English teachers would be proud. And how long did it take you to get back to an attitude of worship after the interruption? A second? Two?" Many nodded.

"That's the true test of faith. It's not that nothing will ever happen to distract us, disrupt us, disturb us to the core. The real issue is how fast we rebound to recover an attitude of worship."

With tears in her eyes, a woman from the audience told me the simple typo in the lyrics brought her more hope than anything she'd been counseled in her crisis. The word picture won't leave her alone. It won't leave me alone either.

Marty and Sonya's story isn't over. Whose ever is? But the headline has changed from *Heartbreaking* to *Inspiring*.

Still difficult but amazing. And life-giving for others whom they now coach to victory.

Just as God must have hoped.

Reflections:

1. Consider the following statement and how it relates to you. Loving when it's least expected is an elegant grace with rich layers of impact—what it does for the loved one, what it does in us, what it communicates to others, and how it moves the heart of God.
2. Guilt aside, what difference might it make in situations

like Sonya's and her husband's to recognize, acknowledge, and vow to be tender with each other's pain?

3. Where does guilt go to die? (See Psalm 32.)

If you know a *Sonya* . . .

The easy thing is avoidance. The second easiest is spewing advice though no one but God truly knows the heart. The hard thing—the best thing—is to plunge right into the hurt with her. Excruciating pain like the kind Sonya knew returns in spasms long after the initial wound is inflicted. How can you let the Sonyas in your life know you haven't forgotten about them, that you care as much now as you ever did?

HIS: So I admitted my sin to you; I didn't conceal my guilt.
"I'll confess my sins to the LORD,*" is what I said.*
Then you removed the guilt of my sin.

PSALM 32:5

HERS: That's why all the faithful should pray to you
during troubled times,
so that a great flood of water won't reach them.
You are my secret hideout! You protect me from trouble.
You surround me with songs of rescue!

PSALM 32:6-7

6. Watching

Charla

SUCH A SIMPLE QUESTION—HOW MANY CHILDREN do you have?

For thirty-two of her forty-eight years, Charla answered with a lie. Her mind counted one more than her mouth reported. A boy no one could know about. A boy she didn't dare think about. A boy who stayed with her even after he had been taken from her arms.

She wasn't supposed to have seen the child. In the delivery room, a blue drape kept her from catching a glimpse. She begged every shift of nurses to let her see him. They'd been instructed to say no. Even the ones who squirmed and looked away when they obeyed the instructions.

Her dad picked her up at the hospital when she was discharged. He didn't speak to her during the hour's drive home.

Charla crawled into bed with an untouchable ache and remained there for three days, not eating, barely drinking, doing little else but crying.

"Just let me see him. I have to see him!" she chanted with a relentlessness that made even the walls nervous.

She knew she couldn't keep the baby. Her parents had more than enough children already. They couldn't afford the physical or emotional costs of raising their teenage daughter's child.

On the fourth day, her dad called her to the kitchen table. He pointed to the newspaper want ads. "Find yourself a job. And a place to live."

Nothing more.

Her mother, staring out the kitchen window as she washed the breakfast dishes, stiffened, but said nothing.

"Mom, please!"

"Charla, do what he says."

The girl crumpled to the floor, the traumas of birth overshadowed by the heart trauma that permeated every other inch of her. "Please let me see him. I just need to see him."

When she opened her eyes, the light was strongest through the west window of the bedroom she shared with four sisters who were, as she should have been, at school. The bedroom door opened with its telltale creak.

"Get dressed and brush your teeth." Her father's words bit through the sorrow like a chain saw through a new scar.

She did as she was told.

Her mother stood waiting in the living room, her massive black purse on one crossed arm. "In the truck," she said.

Charla followed. Her brothers and sisters streamed out of the school bus as the truck edged toward the end of the driveway. Her siblings stared at the three of them in the truck cab but continued down the drive toward the house and the chores that awaited them.

"Where are we going?"

Nothing. No response.

Charla hadn't seen a psychiatric hospital before but imagined it would look just like the dark brick building in front of which her father parked the truck. Feed sacks in the back of the truck still spewed corn dust from the abrupt stop when Charla and her mother exited the passenger side.

A room as hollow as a gymnasium, though a fraction of its size, held a blond wooden crib at the end opposite the door. A crib and a newborn swaddled in blue.

Charla started toward the crib, but her father's arm stopped her.

She leaned against the restraint. "He's crying." Though her body followed instructions, her insides raced across the room, picked up the unhappy child, pressed him to the pain in her breast. Her throat burning, she pleaded, "Let me hold him. Just once."

A suited woman a few feet from the crib, hands clasped in front of her, looked past Charla to her parents and shook her head an inch to the left, an inch to the right.

"You've seen him. Let's go," her mother said, her words pinched and flat.

The sound of the baby's cry mingled with his mother's and followed the trio out the door, down the steps, into the truck, and through the next thirty-two years of Charla's life.

Charla and her parents never spoke of him again.

Like the hum of insects on a summer's night, the baby's cry never ceased, though she learned to carry on around it. She found a room to rent, worked two jobs, and finished school. She avoided most men, but eventually fell in love and married. She held her breath through pregnancies and births, knowing it was irrational but fighting the fear that someone would take the children from her.

The children stayed and grew. The hum remained. As they played in the yard, the words, "You have a half-brother" pressed at the back of her lips, but she swallowed them and carried on.

"How many children do you have, Charla?"

"F—Three."

One day when the hum grew too loud to ignore, she told her husband about the fourth child, the boy with blond hair and a distinct cry. Her husband responded as if he'd known all along, as if hearing the story was not a shock but an explanation for her unspoken but palpable pain.

The married man who'd taken advantage of her sixteen-year-old naiveté created unrelenting emotional distress and a layer of fallout so thick it nearly smothered her. The parents who didn't know how to handle the angst or complications of a teenage mom added another layer.

For more than three decades, Charla couldn't draw a full breath.

Until the day she found her son.

After red tape and letters and phone calls, they met face-to-face in a restaurant.

"You look just like me," she said.

He laughed. He sounded just like her.

Charla clutched at the pain that had settled just beneath her breastbone. "I . . . I didn't know you could laugh."

He'd been adopted by a loving family, raised well, and was content, intelligent, and married, with two boys. No regrets.

Charla had enough regrets for both of them.

No need to apologize. He'd rarely wondered about his birth mom, he confessed. His life was good. When he heard more details of Charla's story, he knew she had not been given a choice. The decisions had been made for her, by people who thought they were doing the right thing.

The plaintive cry from the blond crib across the room had not lasted as long as it had in Charla's mind. He'd been held. Loved. So had she.

Today they're redeeming lost years.

"Four. I have four children," she says, warmed by the truth, by a fourth voice that calls her Mom and by the wonder of restoration.

What do we do with the pain caused by those who thought they were doing the right thing? The parents who make a harsh decision because they don't know what else to do. The friend whose protectiveness hides the truth about your unfaithful spouse so you're caught completely unaware and vulnerable. The instructor who thought he could push you further, misjudging your breaking point. The dad who grew up in an era or culture in which affection equaled weakness.

Without excusing the action or justifying it, we can make peace with it the way Jesus did. "Father, forgive them, for they don't know what they're doing."

Charla's restoration of her soul and of her relationship with her parents began before she found her son. As she accepted the unbending faithfulness of her husband's love and allowed herself to consider the depth of God's love for her, peace preceded her reunion with the baby she'd been forced to give away.

We assume answers are precursors to peace. But answers are all the sweeter when the peace comes first.

Reflections:

1. You may have experienced a similar pattern—that the peace came first, then the answer. To what do you attribute a peace that can't be explained? How does it resemble the peace the apostle Paul talks about in Philippians? "Then the peace of God that exceeds all understanding will keep your hearts and minds safe in Christ Jesus" (Philippians 4:7).

2. Who in your life made choices that have affected you for years, decades? Would they likely make those same decisions today? How will it change your current state of mind if you surrender your memories of their decisions to God's keeping?

3. How is God redeeming what may have once been lost to you?

If you know a *Charla* . . .

If you know a Charla, consider yourself blessed. The restoration of a lost relationship and healing of a chronic wound invigorates those who witness it.

If resolution is still in the longing phase for the *Charla* you know, please be patient with how tender to the touch her wound remains. The smallest breath of memory exacerbates the heart's raw flesh.

I asked Charla to read this chapter after I wrote it. She said, "You captured the pain." Then she added, "It was months after finding my son that I felt the full impact of what God had done for me in giving me another chance with him. For years, I caught myself looking for that unknown face in a crowd. The towheaded boy on the playground, just the right age. Was that him? The youth at the fast-food drive-through window. The young man at the card rack in the grocery store. Could that be him?"

She closed her eyes for a brief moment. "I caught myself wondering one day and realized I didn't have to look anymore."

Mourn with those who mourn, the Bible tells us in Romans 12:15. Rejoice with those who rejoice.

God will make that enough.

He's still in the business of multiplying what little we have—on its own, never enough for the shredded soul—when we bring Him the small loaves and fishes of our compassionate acts.

As a mother comforts her child, so I will comfort you.
ISAIAH 66:13

7. Siphoned Dry

Lorena

HE DIDN'T ROB HER BLIND. SHE WAS LEGALLY blind before he robbed her.

The knock at Lorena's retirement condo that morning could have been FedEx. But it was a federal agent, delivering a message she hadn't considered, much less expected.

"You have nothing left."

"I don't understand."

"Your financial planner . . ."

"Yes. My friend Jerry."

"He's being investigated for investment fraud. You and his other clients are the unfortunate victims of his criminal deception."

Lorena squinted but still couldn't see well enough to read the expression on the man's face, although her magnifying glass assured her his federal agent credentials were genuine. How embarrassed he'd be when he discovered he'd knocked on the wrong door. Jerry had been a cherished friend for decades, part of their social circles. He'd been the first person to call after Lorena's second husband died. Always there to help.

The agent was mistaken.

But, no. He had proof. The modest investments Lorena thought she could count on to carry her through her remaining years were fabrications covering Jerry's sins. He'd not only stolen many hundreds of thousands of dollars from his clients, but had disposed of them in ways that made the lost funds irretrievable. Spent. Gone.

Lorena's disbelief gave way to distress, which quickly morphed into despair.

Comfortably set one minute, she was broke and homeless the next. She'd depended on Jerry to manage her money. Who wouldn't trust such a kind, caring financial planner?

They'd vacationed together when her husband was still alive. Her husband and Jerry played golf together. Jerry always said, "You're in good shape. No worries," when Lorena asked about financial matters after her husband died.

She rarely asked. Although she hadn't been able to work for years, her husband's business had done well. After his death, Jerry's investment expertise guaranteed she could live just as comfortably the rest of her life. A vacation every year. A nice condo in a pleasant neighborhood with the kind of safety and social benefits she needed. A security system. A community room. Shops nearby. Easy access to public transportation, all the more important as her eyesight failed.

Shock led to denial that lasted until the indictment hit the evening news, at which time it handed the controls to devastation, depression, and fear.

Who could blame her for her sense of loss and desperation? The men in her life—her husbands, her son, trusted advisors like Jerry—had always taken care of her. She'd been raised in an era when that was the norm. In her mind, her physical challenges heightened that expectation.

So she'd paid little attention to bank balances, appliance warranties, how much the patio plant irrigation system cost them each month, and where the destitute go when they're in trouble.

Spiritually, as well as financially.

Her church friends were farsighted. They held bake sales and clothing drives for the poor in third world countries, where personal involvement was kept to a minimum. They didn't see the needs of the newly poor in their own community. Uncertain what to do with their Tuesday lunch partner who quit coming because she couldn't afford iced tea, much less a chicken salad croissant, they ignored the rustling inside that said, "We should do something to help." Eventually the feeling faded.

I don't know the end of Lorena's story. I hope someone stepped up to connect her to sources of practical help, to walk her through Crisis Survival Mode, to nurse her through learning how to make do, how to become more independent at a stage in life when the natural swing is toward greater dependence. And I pray she learned when, how, and where to ask for help.

Did she discover that only God can dissolve the bitterness that gnaws at her stomach lining and keeps her from swallowing? Did she find relief from the panic that marked those first days?

I wonder if she opened her Bible to the book of Job and said, "Finally, someone understands," and realized she was talking about both the broken man Job and the sovereign God? Did she clutch the Bible to her chest in the middle of the night as her physical sight continued to fail and her spiritual sight improved?

The choices that brought her financial stability to ruin were not her own, although she probably throttled herself for not staying involved. So in addition to the devastation Jerry brought on by his twisted greed, Lorena would add guilt and embarrassment to the list of topics to discuss with her counselor . . . if she reached out to a counselor.

Others faced with the repercussions of financial fraud report that the gift of a listening ear startled them with its impact. How could knowing someone cares change anything significant? But it does.

On the other side of the tragedy, while still crawling out from under the ash, survivors talk about the benefits of seeing with new eyes—the distinction between items they thought valuable and concepts or relationships they now know truly are. The danger of misplaced pride that sometimes stands in the way of receiving help. The discernment needed to distinguish true and false friends. The importance of moving forward—with a small proactive step—when life looks like one big setback.

How would you survive a financial offense that grave? What if you not only lost your home—as too many people do—but could trace that devastation to the actions of one person? What if it wasn't a series of layoffs and unexpected bills and accumulated debts but an unscrupulous individual who "robbed you blind"?

My husband and I share few similar interests in television viewing. But we both enjoy survival shows, the kind with real vs. reality-TV survivors. We've seen survivors drop onto glaciers with nothing but a single match, or parachute into the jungles of Borneo, or wash ashore on a remote island. I missed the one the other night when two survivors were given nothing but a hundred rolls of duct tape with which to survive until rescue.

One thing successful survivalists have in common is that they spend very little if any time pondering how they got into trouble. They don't gaze disbelievingly at the helicopter from which they dropped, or try to flag down the departing plane for an explanation. They hit the remote beach with a survivor's determination to address the needs of the moment: food, shelter, water, fire. Not always in that order.

If a storm threatens, shelter rises to top priority. But they have to consider where the shelter will be built in light of access to drinkable water and food. If they don't have fire, they can't boil water or get warm or dry out after the storm.

Few make it very far into their adventure if they fail to build a shelter and instead sit on a piece of driftwood, pondering how dark the clouds are growing or how hungry they've become or why their skin doesn't bounce back when they pinch it. "I'm dehydrated!" is a cry that doesn't solve the problem.

"I've been robbed!" A natural initial reaction. But not a survival tactic.

Survivors start with reconnaissance. They don't inventory what they've lost, but what they have at their disposal. What washed up on the beach of their disaster? An old milk jug, a hubcap, and a roll of duct tape? It's a start.

We've seen survivors use a pop-top to fashion a fishhook, steel wool and a battery for a fire starter, and tea made from pine needles. None of those things looked like much. But in the hands of a resourceful person determined to survive, they can be enough.

Lorena thought her life was over when her resources were siphoned off by a supposed friend. I wonder if she found a connection with the God of manna and quail, overflowing oil jars, and masterful creativity. I wonder if she found the cure for bitterness and resentment, or if she's still sitting on a piece of driftwood, looking back on all she's lost.

When my husband and I were first married, lack of financial resources forced us to make do. Orange crates became end tables. A pound of hamburger could stretch for four meals, if we were careful. An old quilt became a wall hanging. Everyone commented on the beauty of the quilt, not knowing it was hung in that spot to cover the bulging plaster in the wall behind it.

Like many of the star-crossed, we assumed life would soon get to the place where we'd no longer have to make do. We have grandchildren now, and we're still making do, still looking for ways to reuse something others might discard, still seeing objects not as items to collect, hoard, accumulate, but as resources, if not for ourselves, then for others.

When economic downturns send the roller-coaster car plummeting to the bottom, we feel the gravitational pull, but not as severely as some, because we've had to be resourceful through the years. We know how to make do.

I watched Lorena plummet, not just because of the crime committed against her financial stability and how lost she felt. Since she hadn't needed to exercise resourcefulness muscles, they'd shriveled. And emotionally, she remained oblivious to the wealth of spiritual resources around her. She didn't know how to tap into the cache of reassurance from a God whom the Bible calls *El Shaddai*—the God Who Is More Than Enough.

She had no real connection to God, so she was unaware of the divine commitment to provide for those in need, especially those victimized by another's actions.

And I? I knew, but failed to tell her.

Reflections:

1. Whether your mate ran up an outrageous credit card bill without your knowledge or your son reneged on his promise to repay the money he borrowed to start his copper wind chime business or you lost your job, house, reputation, and future at the hand of a corporate decision or home intruder, please don't let the despair, however natural, keep you rooted to the driftwood. What's your first survivalist move?

2. What do you have left? A talent unexplored? A survivor's mentality? A caring church family? A community resource center? Family that says, "Let us know if we can help"?

3. Financial ruin is no laughing matter. Have you come out of a crisis like that? What did you discover when you applied yourself to the mission of recon? What bits and pieces do you have to work with . . . in addition to the innovation and creativity of a God who cares about you?

If you know a *Lorena* . . .

As I wrote this chapter, remembering when I was told this story, a fourteen-foot wave of empathy washed over me. That poor woman! Then a second wave hit. What did I do about her crisis? I remember writing a note in the early days of devastation. She might not have had the strength to read notes then, despite my writing in large print out of consideration for her eyesight limitations. Thoughtful, right?

But what did I tangibly do to ease her burden? It doesn't matter that she was merely a friend of a friend and not someone I was accustomed to talking to or even praying for. She hurt and I watched from the security of my well-built shelter.

I could have sent her a grocery gift card. I could have researched help centers in her area. I could have called to let her know somebody cared, even if I didn't have the means to pay the rent on her condo.

It takes courage to pray, "Lord, make me more sensitive to the financial needs around me. And show me what I already have that can make a difference in that person's life."

Be strong! Be fearless! Don't be afraid and
don't be scared by your enemies
because the LORD *your God is the*
one who marches with you.
He won't let you down, and he won't abandon you.
DEUTERONOMY 31:6

8. A Thousand Bad Decisions

Max

TWO MINUTES. THREE, MAYBE. THESE THINGS HAD to move quickly. He'd be in and out of the house before Denny could count to a hundred. The kid *could* count to . . .

Sure, he could.

Max tucked the package deeper into the pocket of his hoodie. Why did Denny have to show up and complicate things? Max pointed two fingers toward him from his place behind the wheel. "Dude, don't follow me. Wait here in the car. No matter what."

All he needed was Denny's mama on his back for contributing to the delinquency of a—

Well, Denny wasn't a minor anymore. But still. He was about as street smart as a graham cracker. What did he want a life like this for, anyway? Denny had it good at home, despite his old man. He had a home.

Max shot him a look that punctuated his warning, then exited the car. He took in the scene.

A couple of other parked cars on the street, unoccupied.

A mangy, three-legged dog relieving himself on a telephone pole.

Sorry yards. Sagging porch steps. Stashes of empty beer bottles no one would mistake for lawn art.

Adrenalin-fired, he reined in his urge to beeline it for the tar-papered house in the middle of the block, four houses from where they'd parked. He sauntered, forcing himself to breathe in the practiced pattern.

Two taps on the weathered, windowless door were followed by a squeal of tires behind him. He knew that sound. Before the door opened in front of him, he turned and dropped to the pavement, gun drawn. As he rolled in the stubbly grass toward an abandoned recliner barricade, he heard the pop of gunfire.

A shapeless black vehicle screeched past him, rounded the corner without stopping, and disappeared.

Why hadn't they fired on him? Finished him off? He'd been out in the open long enough.

Denny.

Curtains parted a millimeter and window-blind slats spread an inch up and down the street. Max stuck his gun into his waistband and crouch-ran to his car.

The passenger window, splatted with blood, told the story. Denny's head—eyes open but unseeing—lolled against the cracked glass. No!

Max opened the door cautiously, bracing Denny's limp body against his side until he could reach in and pull him out. He collapsed onto the curb with Denny bleeding in his arms. Shot in his left temple. Denny hadn't even turned to look before the drive-by gunman aimed through the driver's side window.

"Man, I told you not to follow me. I told you I was bad news." Max groaned and mopped at the wound with the cuff of his hoodie. "Why don't you ever listen to me?"

Denny answered with a moan and gurgle, his last breath.

Max slumped lower in his chair, exhausted from relating the years-old story.

"There's more, isn't there?" I calculated the time it would have taken for the cops and an ambulance to show up, the "package" still in his pocket, the gun in his waistband, the men in one of the houses still waiting for a delivery they weren't about to dismiss.

"I'll tell you another day, maybe."

"You weren't the shooter," I offered. Pale comfort.

"I might as well have been. Denny wouldn't have been there if it weren't for me."

Years separate Max from the tragedy. Years. Jail. Repentance. Forgiveness. Restoration. His life now bears little resemblance to the one memorialized by that bloody curb scene. But the visual is imprinted on his brain.

"A thousand bad decisions on my part," he said. "One on his. I told him, 'Dude, whatever you do, don't follow *me*.' "

"What would you tell him today, Max, if you could?"

He rubbed his palms on the thighs of his jeans. Then he flipped open his ragged hope—his worn and tattered Bible. Hunks of pages fell out. He stuffed them back in and kept looking. "Here," he said, pointing to a fingerprinted page. "I'd tell him, 'Follow me as I follow Christ.'"

Denny's parents keened their way through the first few years after their son's senseless death. They eventually forgave Max for the part he played. God had been ready to forgive Max long before he asked. But the nightmares remained.

He can face it now, talk about it now, because he's learning how to show himself mercy. He once thought clinging to the nightmares was the least he could do, out of respect for his friend and the pain he'd caused Denny's family.

But the nightmares kept him rooted to past mistakes, tethered to past sins. Kept him focused on his life before redemption entered the picture.

"That's who you *were*," I reminded him. "Who are you now?"

For years Max straddled two truths—what he'd done and what he'd been forgiven. He walked with a spiritual limp when he leaned on his past. Then a subtle shift in his thinking pressed him a few degrees forward. Positioned that way, progress met less resistance. He began to log more wise choices than not. He established a pattern of behavior that left no room for regret. And he grew to care about how his actions affected others and the God who'd rescued him.

Max isn't stingy with grace toward others. He moves through his new life with a sharp, acute attentiveness to the needs of those least likely to feel worthy of mercy. The challenge he faces today, he says, is holding his plate still, not yanking it away, as God ladles out more and more grace for him.

"Who are you *now*, Max?" I repeated.

"Someone . . . worth . . . following?"

"Is God merciful?" I asked the broken woman sitting in the chair across from me between sessions at a conference.

She tugged at the loose thread on the arm of the chair. "Yes." Tentative, but audible.

"One of the people who most needs it is you."

"But . . ."

"Show yourself some mercy. God does."

With Max, Denny's choice to walk right into danger cost him his life and loaded Max with even more regret. Max's long list of regrettable choices of his past life negatively affected more people than he can count. When he tries, the nightmares resurface.

Should he be required to pay a price in nightmares in addition to the prison time he's served? Some would say yes.

God says, "Hand 'em over. Mercy covers nightmares, too."

Whether the victim, the perpetrator, or an innocent bystander, we can count on heaven's tagline: *There's an app of mercy for that.*

Reflections:

1. A friend died in Max's arms, and wouldn't have if Max made other choices. A baby dies in its parents' arms, and they're in anguish over their choice not to risk surgery. A wife breathes her last and her husband regrets their decision about chemotherapy. The outcomes seem tied to a single choice, launching a lifetime of regret.

   But many sorrows are a reflection of a much longer history than a single choice. In your own situation, can you trace back to "So, that's where it all started"?

2. How do you respond to the Scripture that tells us Jesus was a "man of sorrows"—plural—"acquainted with deepest grief" (Isaiah 53:3 NLT)? If it doesn't comfort you, can you describe why it doesn't?

3. In Max's application, the word redemption overlaps most dictionary meanings. Deliverance. Rescue. Atonement for guilt. Repurchase, as of something bought back.

God and God's grace bought back a tormenting memory, reclaimed it for holier purposes. Has the same happened for you?

If you know a *Max* . . .

When Max tells his story, he always includes a poignant scene that he credits as a grab-him-by-the-shoulders-and-turn-him-around moment.

Imprisoned for numerous crimes and misdemeanors, he spent the better part—the *better* part—of seventeen years behind bars. At the end of himself, and after exhausting most rehab systems and twelve-step programs, he sat in jail again. A short sentence, but cripplingly boring and devoid of hope.

And someone visited him.

Someone who loved God and loved Max and started Max thinking that what God offered might be true and possible not just for others but for him. Mercy. Forgiveness. Life.

The visitor wasn't gifted in prison ministry. It didn't even make his list of "things I'd consider doing for Jesus." But he was moved to visit Max that day. And he abandoned himself and his fears to flat-out obey.

Is someone's turning point waiting for you to abandon your hesitation?

———

Follow my example, just like I follow Christ's.
1 CORINTHIANS 11:1

9. If Only I'd Known

Catherine

"YOU SAID HE WAS DEAD."

"He is now."

Catherine slammed the law office envelope on the table. Her mother paused in her task only long enough for one stroke of the potato peeler. Catherine's insides smoldered. "That's not funny."

"He never was."

"Look at me! You knew Dad was alive? All this time?"

Eva dropped the peeler into the sink, dried her hands on a

towel, and turned to face her daughter, the livid one. "You wouldn't have liked him."

"How would I know? I wasn't given the chance to find out." Scalding tears took the steam out of her voice, but the passion remained. "You said he left us. But you kicked him out."

Eva's jawline tightened. Her hands knotted. "What does it matter now?"

"All these years, I thought he didn't care about me. Then when I pestered you for an address so I could contact him, you . . . you made up a story that he'd died? Who does that? What kind of bitter woman would—?"

"Oh, grow up. You're thirty years old. Get over it."

Catherine snatched the lawyer's letter from the table and turned to leave the kitchen. She stopped at the archway to the dining room and swung around to face her mother. "I understand that you and he couldn't get along. But you didn't give me a chance to see if he and I could. And now it's too late."

On the drive to her apartment, Catherine mentally raced through thirty fatherless years, wondering what it would have been like to know she was loved. If the letter his lawyer sent represented his true heart, her dad had missed her as intensely as she'd missed him.

She'd mourned his so-called death when she was thirteen and searching. All those years she could have tried to make contact. All those years she grieved over a man who lived, but she was unaware. If the lawyer hadn't tracked her down, would she ever have known the truth?

The disgust she felt for her mother's deception forced her to the side of the road. She put the car in park, laid her head on the steering wheel, and cried three decades worth of tears.

What right did her mother have to withhold the truth from her? That singular decision might have saved her years of abandonment therapy, the kind that comes in cartons of Häagen-Dazs ice cream.

Maybe her mother had been trying to protect her. But from what? Since the arrival of the death notice—the genuine one—and the lawyer's notes and letters, she'd learned her dad was a great guy with a loving family, father to Catherine's unknown half-sisters. She had sisters!

Whatever ugliness destroyed his relationship with Catherine's mother, it hadn't followed him into his future.

Now a fatal heart attack had removed all hope of her reconnecting with him. Maybe he wouldn't have wanted to establish a father-daughter relationship with her. But she deserved to know the truth about him.

Jaw clenched, hands gripped tight on the motionless steering wheel, she prayed a three-word universal prayer. "God, help me."

A thought teased the edges of her brain. She would not become a second generation of bitter women in her family. Her mother had a lock on that. Catherine had grieved at thirteen. She'd grieve again now. But she wouldn't become a younger version of the kind of woman who lets past hurts make her heart brittle.

Her grip on the steering wheel loosened. She'd mirrored her mother in many positive ways. But in this respect, she would not conform to the pattern.

She'd fully embrace her loss. She'd always regret what might have been. But responding as her mother had when Catherine was a child could only give birth to more pain. They'd had enough of that to last a lifetime.

The prayer repeated itself as she pulled the car back onto the road. "God, help me."

The fallout of other people's destructive choices becomes more toxic, more suffocating, when our response is equally caustic. We don't climb out of an ash heap by piling on more ash.

Sages would chant, "Two wrongs don't make a right." The Bible words it this way: "Don't pay back evil for evil or insult for insult. Instead, give blessing in return" (1 Peter 3:9).

Not natural. Not easy. Not expected. Not deserved.

How? A constant repetition of the universal three-word prayer: "God, help me."

Reflections:

1. Somewhere in the mire of her own disappointment and anguish, Catherine's mother Eva made a decision: her daughter didn't need to know the truth. She was better off without it. Whether embittered or misguided or overprotective or a combination of the three, Eva's choice carved

a deep scar in Catherine's young life. One of the most courageous actions we can take is ending a toxic pattern. Catherine determined not to repeat or reflect how she'd been treated. Her choice involved a much healthier response—forgiveness. What generational pattern have you worked hard to interrupt? How successful have you been?

2. Has Catherine's short prayer—*God, help me!*—passed your lips? What were the circumstances? How did God answer? What is your confidence level about a prayer like that receiving a response?

3. Psalm 22:24 records the songwriter David's "God, help me!" prayer and the response he received.

> He [God] didn't despise or detest the suffering of the one
>   who suffered—
> he didn't hide his face from me.
> No, he listened when I cried out to him for help.

The Psalms resonate with many who appreciate the author's honesty and the fact that many of the songs were penned in stressful times, in the middle of some of life's gravest disappointments. In what way do you think Catherine or others like her could benefit from expressing herself—pain and all—on paper?

If you know a *Catherine* . . .

Who could put a price on the value of a listening ear, of having someone to listen when life spills over and leaves a mess? As Catherine develops new ways of carrying her pain, she may appreciate a friend who will listen to her imagination's journey through the lost years. I want to be that person for the Catherines I know. Do you? We'll need reserves of time and patience. God, help us.

Save me by your power and answer me
so that the people you love might be rescued.
PSALM 108:6

10. Hope Hackers

Neil

DEAR IDENTITY THIEF,

I know you thought this was fun, but could I have my life back?

Swiping my identity gained you access to my friends—who won't believe the things you're saying, by the way—and what looks like several expensive coffee drinks, a new camera case, and tickets to a concert you may or may not have enjoyed.

Here's what it cost me.

I had to change all my passwords and apologize to all my e-mail and social network friends.

I had to apologize *profusely* to my business acquaintances who were affected by your hacking "cough."

I spent an hour and a half, three days in a row, working with my credit card company to figure out which charges were mine and which were yours. My compliments to your taste in vacation destinations.

I can't order the tickets for my own vacation until the mess is cleared up with the credit card company.

I had to get a new cell phone number, which is not the same number as the one on my recently printed business cards.

My boss called me into the office to ask why I was sending him morally objectionable material via e-mail. I'm not sure I convinced him you were the pervert, not me.

Oh, yes. The mortgage for our new home is on hold with the bank because of what you did to my credit report. Closing was supposed to be next Monday. The real estate agents are trying to work it out, but patience is wearing thin.

Thank you for the learning experience of the night in jail. Although I wasn't afforded the blessing of paying for your crimes in full after being arrested for something on your rap sheet, the night behind bars deepened my commitment to support those in prison ministry . . . when my bank accounts are unfrozen.

My passport application is in limbo. I hope you don't mind, but I'm forwarding all complaints from the short-term mission team to the address you stole.

Sincerely,

Neil Brooks, the Original

Neil expressed his angst in sarcasm—writing an imaginary letter to his identity thief. The sense of violation Neil felt was tempered by his clever sense of humor. But some who fall prey to an identity thief's crimes and the havoc of the aftermath find recovery overwhelming.

"There's another thing . . . and another . . . and another!"

Identity theft unleashes chaos that drags on for months or longer.

Emotionally, the toll can be high for identity theft victims as well. How easy it seemed to lose who they were—a click of a hacker's computer mouse.

Though we can hope hackers will always be caught, thieves always punished, reality tells us that's not the case. Too often, the victim pays more heavily than the perpetrator.

The incident makes the innocent more cautious, more diligent to change passwords frequently and keep track of what's happening in their bank accounts, increasing safety measures and installing stronger security systems.

But beyond that, what's next? What else can a person do? And how does one turn the corner from a sense of vulnerability to a position of strength?

In the aftermath of the identity theft violation, Neil proactively did what he could to make life tough for the next identity thief. Practical actions—password changes, firewall adjustments, changes in his purchasing habits.

That took care of the external issues.

He also turned to passages like Psalm 37 and read that the day is coming when the wicked will get what they deserve. "The LORD won't leave the righteous to the power of the wicked," reads Psalm 37:33.

How do we carry on, knowing we live in a world where bad people who seem devoid of consciences take advantage of innocents?

"Hope in the LORD and keep his way!" reads Psalm 37:34. "When the wicked are eliminated, you will see it for yourself!"

Anger growls as if it wields power, a noisy Chihuahua emotion. The truth is it drains us of the ability to effect positive change. Releasing our hold on anger restores us to a place of strength.

Anger does not have to hold us in its grip. We're the ones with fingers tightened around it. We think and act as if we have no control, that it controls us. It may feel that way. But we are not its helpless victims.

Like a teacher with a recalcitrant student, we look into that defiant face and in essence say, "I know you're assigned to my classroom for this school term. You're here. But you *will* behave, and you will sit where I tell you to sit, there in the corner, where you won't disturb the rest of the room."

That's a gross oversimplification. But maybe our natural tendency is to overcomplicate it.

My husband and I sat among other mourners at a funeral for a young man's mother. She'd been murdered by her boyfriend. The shock of it ripped through the community and tore through the young man's heart. "I don't know what to do with my anger," he said. "I don't know what to do with it."

A man of strong, vibrant faith, he wasn't immune from choking, knee-buckling anger. Repulsed by its presence, he wanted to find a place to put it where he wouldn't be so aware of it, every step weighed down by it.

He may have expected not to feel anger. But that would have made him less than human.

The anger didn't lift in an instant. It faded. The less attention he gave it, the less it pulsed. The paler it grew. He loosened his grip on his right to be angry about the senselessness and utter horror of the act that cost his mother's life. He surrendered his need for revenge to his God, who does a much better job of it.

As his fingers unclenched, anger weakened in power.

Few of us will deal with an anger caused by a grief of that magnitude. But we share common ground, no matter how large or small the inciting incident.

In Neil's case, while climbing out from under the fallout of the identity theft, he discovered that the most brilliant hacker with the power to wreak havoc with our personal information is no match for the God who reserves the right to exact revenge on our behalf.

Anger dissipated as he scribbled the word *retribution* on God's to-do list and erased it from his own.

Reflections:

1. In Gideon's time in the Bible (Judges 7:20), the army entered a battle—in which they knew themselves to be inexpressibly vulnerable—with one hand on their God-praiser trumpets and one hand on their lamps, which both literally and symbolically threw light on the scene. They emerged, by God's intervention, resounding victors. How does that relate to recovery from identity theft?

2. In Nehemiah's time, the people rebuilt their future "with a load [of materials] in one hand and a weapon in the other" (Nehemiah 4:17). They succeeded in their task because they were alert, observant, and applied themselves to their God-appointed assignment. What's your reaction to the common ground in those two stories?

3. Consider the following statements:

   Focusing on the perpetrator is not worth the time spent.

   Focusing on retaliation or retribution—almost always impossible anyway—only serves to exhaust us.

   Focusing on recovery is the only exercise worth the effort.

If you know a *Neil* . . .

Almost all the practical labor of recovering from an incidence of identity theft is the responsibility of the person who was wronged. There's no way around it. Only through.

But having a friend who empathizes with the sense of violation lightens the labor. Knowing someone understands the misery inflicted quiets some of the spasms.

In this and other violations, hearing a "Well, if you think that's bad, listen to this!" I-can-do-you-one-worse story deflates rather than builds up. Your tale of woe may be more dramatic. The person living in violation's aftermath doesn't need more drama. Weigh carefully whether your story needs to be told at all right now.

Rescue me from the grip of the wrongdoer
and the oppressor
because you are my hope, Lord.
PSALM 71:4-5

11. Rest Insured

Tia

THE SERENE VALLEY FUNERAL HOME NEEDED A new name, in Tia's opinion. The word *Valley*, they could keep. Fitting. But *Serene* bordered on prosecutable false advertising.

The funeral director's molasses-thick and just as dark voice was supposed to evoke serenity, calm, sympathy. But the process he proposed raised Tia's heart rate and made her palms sweat.

You need Dustin's obituary by four o'clock? Today? A few hours ago, we were packing for vacation. I have flight numbers and motel reservations in my head. Not aneurisms and obituaries.

She'd asked if he remembered to pack socks. No response. At first, she'd thought his melodramatic collapse over his open suitcase a slightly over-the-top passive-aggressive complaint about her attention to detail. But he didn't move. Ever. Not under his own power.

The paramedics buzzed over his body with IV tubing and resuscitation efforts before loading him into the ambulance, but Tia knew before they told her that he was gone.

"Where do you want his body taken?" the trauma center nurse asked her when the last of the machines were silenced.

"What do you mean?"

The nurse patted Tia's hand. "Your funeral home of choice."

People as young as Tia and Dustin didn't discuss their "choice" of funeral homes. The subject hadn't come up.

Except once. A commercial on television caught her eye. "Nice landscaping," she thought. Tasteful landscaping had to mean something. So she answered the nurse, "Serene Valley?"

The nurse tapped something into her computer tablet. "Good."

What did she mean by that? Tia second-guessed her decision. What if she blew it and picked a funeral home Dustin would have hated? Not that it mattered to him anymore.

Too many miles of highway and skyway stood between Tia and the family that would arrive later. The obituary task lay on her shoulders alone.

Tia's stomach roiled at the anger she felt toward her officially late husband for leaving her in this predicament. He was the one good with words.

She brushed aside hot tears as she pulled open file drawers and shuffled through papers, looking for the precise details about his "preceded in death by," his college fraternity, his work experience, his life before they met. A folder tab caught her eye. "Life Insurance Policy."

Another set of words she didn't anticipate needing for a couple of decades.

She pulled the file and set it on the desk to attend to later, after she figured out how to describe her husband in newspaper language.

Two sets of obituaries turned in—a short version for immediate use and a longer version for the full obit (how nice that those things were now online for the world to see) and the funeral—Tia opened the life insurance file.

She remembered signing the policy, but as particular as she normally was about details, she couldn't remember dollar amounts or the answer to "What now?"

Inside the folder was a stamped, self-addressed envelope. Unsealed but plump. The stamp was in a denomination from two postal increases ago.

Dustin hadn't mailed the policy.

Tia hadn't questioned. She assumed the life insurance premium was one of their automatic withdrawal payments each month, things that fell under the list of Dustin's responsibilities.

Maybe he'd filed electronically. Maybe the policy was active and intact. He wouldn't have neglected something that important. He couldn't have.

What she made as a teacher's aide would never cover the mortgage. Her salary took care of things like birthday gifts and the vacation they were packing for when Dustin decided to leave her. The hard way.

The pulse in her temples throbbed, distorting her vision with each beat. On the other side of town, a mortician worked on Dustin's cold body. As if her grief had distorted her cognitive powers, all she could think about was that he'd forgotten to stick the life insurance policy in the mail.

Scream Valley Funeral Home.

A more fitting name.

Widows survive without life insurance. Tia's age worked in her favor. If her health held, she had decades of working years ahead of her, and she loved her job. It wasn't the lost income, or the lost potential to pay off the house, or the help Dustin's life insurance would have provided for the kids' college or for the shocking funeral fees.

Rational or not, Tia wrestled with an emotional loss—
bordering on betrayal—that compounded her grief over losing Dustin and wrestled with guilt that the thought even
crossed her mind.

When they'd talked to the agent about life insurance,
Dustin balked at the cost of the premiums but claimed it was
important to him to provide for her and the kids if anything
happened to him.

Had he changed his mind?

No. It was an oversight. That's all. It didn't represent anything more than simple forgetfulness.

Within minutes, her mind would drift where she didn't
want it to go. If he cared, wouldn't he have made sure she
and the kids were taken care of?

What was it that kept Dustin from following through? The
papers were signed. He'd gotten as far as stamping the envelope, years ago. Why hadn't he licked the glue and stuck the
envelope in the mail?

Her hope that he'd filed electronically crumbled when she
investigated further, making calls she had no time or heart to
make. She vacillated from blaming her now-buried husband
to blaming herself for not paying more attention. Once an
initial decision is made, who gives life insurance a second
thought?

Like a dust cloud on a gravel road, guilt and resentment
tumbled behind her. Dustin was a good man who rarely
messed up, but her memories of their years together ended

with a mental postscript about the one thing he forgot to do. Like someone instructed to think about anything but pineapple, all she could think about was that one thing. And she despised herself for it.

A stew that simmers contentedly creates a rich, satisfying broth. But if it boils dry, it's no longer edible.

Dustin's oversight may have set off a chain reaction of problems, may have started the pot bubbling. But Tia's obsession with the incident and its very real but unchangeable consequences boiled it dry.

When I get to thinking too nobly about myself, confident that I don't bear grudges—*Thank You, Jesus!*—a scene from my childhood takes center stage in my mind. A small moment that formed an indelible memory.

The risk I'm taking to tell you about it sobers me. Such a small thing. How could it have bothered me enough then to file it in the "forever" folder? What would cause it to stay with me all these years when other far more important things have faded? Maybe it's there to remind me how close I walk to the edge of grudge-holding.

My sisters and I shared a bedroom at the time; the boys shared another. Three of us girls, eleven and under, with just enough to get by and few trinkets to dust. But I had one—a white porcelain dog about four inches tall. It sat on the tall dresser we girls shared.

Mom asked Dad to move the dresser to the other side of

the room. Eager to get the job done and progress to other projects, Dad started pushing the dresser across the bare hardwood.

"Dad, let me get my dog off there. I don't want it to fall."

"It'll be fine," he said.

But it wasn't. Before he'd finished the sentence, the dog had toppled off the dresser onto the hard floor. Although in reality I probably had others, I remember it as my *one* treasure. It lay in shards.

My dad was a good dad, easy to forgive. It was an accident, unintentional, although, if he'd listened to me . . .

Why would that incident stick with me? Why can I see it playing out in my mind, although the list of sacrifices he and Mom made for me over the years dwarf that small, insignificant loss? I can't even remember if the porcelain dog was a poodle or a cocker spaniel, who gave it to me, or why I cared.

I hope that memory sticks with me to keep me humbled— that no matter how mature I get—someday—or how strong my faith grows, I'm as vulnerable as anyone else to pettiness, to placing too much stock in something not worth the brain storage.

A shattered trinket changed nothing long-term for me. What if it was a small oversight that *had* changed everything? How would I have responded?

Tia's healing began the day she determined not to give her husband's oversight more weight than it deserved, more brain storage than she could afford. Thinking about it, analyzing what it might have meant to her husband's subconscious couldn't change the outcome.

So she stopped giving the unmailed envelope attention and instead ceremoniously gave it a burial.

Reflections:

1. Imagine a seemingly small oversight that changes every moment of someone's future. Is that your story? How often does the other person's negligence creep into your thought patterns?
2. Golfers are told to "play it where it lies," to make the best of where the golf ball lands, no matter the obstacles or inconvenience. Unless they opt for a penalty stroke or strokes, they find a way over, around, or through the hindrances in their way. Fair or not, how does a play-it-where-it-lies attitude change things for someone paying the price for another person's oversight?
3. It would be unkind to fail to acknowledge that some oversights or negligence can cost a lot more than a life insurance payout. A doctor dismisses the smudge on the x-ray. A mom turns her back for a split second. A father in a hurry backs over his three-year-old's tricycle . . . and his three-year-old.

   "But I didn't mean to."

   "It was an accident."

"I'll never forgive myself."

What does a grieving person do with the offender's regret?

If you know a *Tia* . . .

Reminding her of her husband's failure is no more comforting than ignoring her husband's failure.

"These things happen." It's one of those lines that both comforts and irritates. Yes, these things happen. When they happen to us, a flip response trivializes the very real impact on our lives.

So, when we're the ones standing by when "these things" happen to others, what are our options?

a. If you can't say something nice, don't say anything at all.—Mother

b. Be kind one to another.—God

c. Don't say anything at all. We're not obligated to offer a response other than the assurance that we care. The smartest human lacks the IQ to pick perfect words when words get in the way.

If her task is picking up the pieces and reconfiguring her future, our job is to find the delicate balance of knowing when to empathize and when to motivate, when to listen and when to act, when to give advice and when to step back. According to Ecclesiastes, there's a time for both.

There's a season for everything
and a time for every matter under the heavens . . .
a time for planting and a time for uprooting
what was planted . . .
a time for tearing down and a time for building up . . .
a time for keeping and a time for throwing away,
a time for tearing and a time for repairing,
a time for keeping silent and a time for speaking . . .
—FROM ECCLESIASTES 3

12. Baby, Don't Go

Alicia

"DON'T GO, RICK. STAY HOME TONIGHT. WE'LL finish the thank-you notes for the wedding gifts. I'll make popcorn."

He shrugged into his jacket and grabbed the keys from the hook by the kitchen door. "I won't be out long."

"Rick?"

The slump of his shoulders told her he knew what was coming. But she had to say it. "No drinking, okay?"

The door closed on his tight words. "No problem, Babe. I'll have milk." He laughed.

After that night, three months into their marriage, he didn't drink again for almost a year. Everything he ingested came through a feeding tube or an IV site.

The thank-you notes lost their priority in light of caregiving for Alicia's invalid husband. The blush of young love turned to the fever of infection risk, medication cocktails, and a series of surgeries to rebuild Rick's face, femurs, and most of his internal structure.

No amount of surgery could rebuild their relationship. It looked nothing like what they'd shared the day they'd danced—tuxedoed and gowned—to the strains of "I Will Always Love You" and the applause of family and friends.

"He could have stayed home that night," she told me. "He could have decided not to drink. Not to drive. He could have called me to come get him. Now everything's . . ."

I waited for her to catch her breath and finish her sentence. Changed? Different? Harder? Impossible?

"Empty."

Young and in love turned to young and in debt. Young and in the hospital. Young and at physical therapy. Young and upended.

Their newlywed apartment turned handicap accessible with a hospital bed, hydraulic lift, and commode.

The tropical honeymoon they'd postponed until the hurricane season passed became the honeymoon they'd take if

Rick ever walked again, and if they ever climbed out of the medical debts not covered by their inadequate health insurance. The hurricane hit . . . at home.

Rick's medical leave from the paper mill ran out before he regained consciousness. Within days of the accident, Alicia quit grad school and took an uninspiring job. A graduate degree in medieval literature no longer held her attention and might never pay their mounting bills.

Alicia's schedule no longer allowed for Thursday lunch with her girlfriends or leisurely Saturday mornings lingering over a cup of coffee and a favorite book. Rick's need for total care rubbed her vow "for better or for worse, in sickness . . ." tissue-paper thin and rough as burlap. It consumed every hour she wasn't at work. The home health aides consumed every dollar she earned at work.

Three years later, she sat beside me after a speaking engagement, working hard to subdue the sobs that shook her shoulders and clogged her sinuses. "He's doing better," she said. "He's healing. I can't say the same for our marriage. And I . . . I think it's my fault."

I listened to her story, to the ways her husband's personality had changed, to the reasons for the exhaustion etched on her young face. She'd been faithful to him, kind to him, dedicated to his care. When would she reach the part in her story where she'd reveal the awful thing she'd done to their marriage?

She rehearsed the night she'd begged him to stay home

with her, not to go out drinking with his still-learning-the-meaning-of-the-word-*responsible* buddies. "Rick did this to us," she said. "He's the reason our dreams are as crushed as the bones in his face."

The words hung in the air between us.

"But I can't forget it was his decision that night that made things the way they are today. He didn't only change *his* life forever. He changed mine. And our marriage. I didn't realize until now that my silent blame makes every task harder, every challenge that much more difficult."

I put my arm around her as the last of her sobs quieted.

"He's my husband. I'm going to take care of him no matter whose fault it was. I'm going to love him no matter what shape he's in or what wrong decisions got him there." She drew in a broken breath. "I'm not helping either one of us by focusing on how mad I am that he did such a dumb thing. What you said in your talk helped me see that."

I mentally thumbed through my notes. What had I said? What had renewed her hope? It might have been this: *When love's working right, mercy always gets the last word.*

Belaboring the cause of the accident served no purpose. Rehearsing the reason for their distress drained what small reserves of energy she had. Alicia grasped hold of a significant game changer for them as a couple. It didn't matter whose fault it was. Resentment negates grace. Their apartment was too small to let resentment bunk there one more day.

Softness edged her voice as she symbolically laid down her right to be angry over how Rick's decisions changed their lives.

Subtle changes in her routine surprised her with their impact. She accepted the respite care she'd resisted and spent the downtime on soul-refreshing activities like a visit to the botanical gardens, the historical museum, the art show. She took a book and a thermal container of tea to a bench in the park, disengaging from her caregiving for two hours that cleared her lungs and her head.

Nearly exhausted from praying for his healing, Alicia changed tactics to thank God for another day with him. At first, the words sounded rusty, like water from an unused pipe. Then the water cleared.

One day she caught herself humming as she shaved the stubble from Rick's face. His eyes brightened and he mouthed, "I will always love you, too."

Now what? Life is changed forever. We can't recapture permanently altered dreams. Alicia and her husband—no matter how much effort they invested—couldn't go back to the moment prior to his decision to leave the house that night. No do-overs allowed for a life-ripping choice like that.

So, let's label our marriage Traumatized, because it's true. And let's keep that label only. No other.

Or . . .

Traumatized, but Healing. Changed, but Gaining Momentum. Altered Forever, and Learning to Walk Again.

An engaged couple—each party with baggage to spare—hit a rocky patch last week. "It's not the big things," the groom-to-be confessed. "We're doing okay there. It's the little things."

So often true.

My husband fell fifteen feet from a tree and morphed from tall, dark, and handsome to prone, pale, and broken. An accident. No one's fault. But the fallout of the fall changed our lives temporarily. I say "temporarily" with hope in my voice, since we're still in the middle of it. Lost wages. Medical chaos. Complete caregiving.

His broken femur and broken back will heal, the doctors assure us. They also caution us to expect progress to seem excruciatingly slow. It is.

It's the small choices we're making in this season that add a sweetness to the sour stew of unpleasant reality. Smiling when we feel like sighing. Fierce determination to appreciate one another and make our appreciation obvious. Valuing the imposed excess of togetherness. My hands gentle as I wash his hair for him. His words gentle as he prays over me.

Alicia sang while she worked. He needed her help and thanked her for it. She saw tenderness in his eyes. He heard tenderness in her voice. He gave her space to be her whole self. She gave him time to learn how to express his love.

I have hope for them. I have hope for us. It's in the little things.

Reflections:

1. When would starting a discussion with "Things would be different for us if you hadn't . . ." serve a worthwhile purpose? How do you see the statement "resentment negates grace" playing out in your life?

2. Under what circumstances would labling blame change things for the better? In light of what you've been forgiven, ask yourself the question again.

3. Complete the following sentence. Whose fault it is doesn't matter anymore. What matters is _____

_____.

If you know an *Alicia* . . .

For people bearing a long-term burden, with no end in sight, it's easy to get lost in the consuming nature of circumstances. The Bible tells us those who rest in God find new reserves of strength and find the spent strength from the previous day revived. In what way can you help hurting ones renew their energies?

Long after the initial fevered pitch of the introduction of the crisis, can you volunteer as caregiver for a day and tuck a spa gift certificate in your friend's hand? What would it do to her spirits to be included in a conversation about something other than medical issues? Can you and your friends band together to purchase respite care for a weekend? Are you attentive to their financial and emotional needs for the long haul, for better or for worse?

The one who is high and lifted up,
who lives forever, whose name is holy, says:
I live on high, in holiness,
and also with the crushed and the lowly,
reviving the spirit of the lowly,
reviving the heart of those who have been crushed.

ISAIAH 57:15

13. Truth Be Told

Deena

"WHERE WERE YOU . . . REALLY?"

Pam looked up from her cell phone screen. "At the car wash. Really."

"Okay." Deena's word—that *okay* with so many meanings depending on the inflection—hung cloud-like between them.

"What's up with the interrogation? I got stuck in the line at the car wash. Something must have gone goofy with the sprayer arm. I'm next in line, but the vehicle inside the building isn't moving. The cars behind me are tight on my bumper, so I can't just back out. And then an attendant comes and fiddles with the controls, but still nothing. That's when I called you to say I'd be late."

"I didn't get a message."

Pam laid her phone on the table and stirred sweetener into her coffee. "Didn't leave one. The wash door opened then and let me in. I knew it would be just a few more min—" She frowned. "Deena, what's the deal? Are you calling me a liar? I was stuck at the car wash. Five minutes late. That's not bad, considering."

Deena fidgeted. She opened her mouth to say something, then closed it again, lips pressed into a pale line.

"Talk to me, Deena. I wouldn't lie to you. I'm not making this up."

"I know."

"Then . . ."

With her gaze locked on the untouched grilled chicken salad in front of her, Deena said, "I've been lied to my whole life. The truth is a . . . a foreign language . . . and I only recognize a few basic words."

Pam slipped her fingers through the generous handle on her coffee mug. Solid. Dependable. Deena hadn't known anyone she could count on. Pam intended to do what she could to change that.

"Friends don't lie, if they want to stay friends."

"Now, there's a true statement." Deena pressed out an A-for-effort smile. "My dad lied to me without flinching. I used to watch my mom's shoulders to see if they twitched when he spoke. That was my signal not to believe what he was saying."

"I'm so sorry."

"Not your fault. I'm the one with the problem." She stabbed her fork through a chunk of chicken and a lettuce leaf. "I have, as they say, 'trust issues.'"

Pam swirled her spoon through her clam chowder. "And I have anger issues."

"You? Angry?"

"It makes me furious that the choices your dad made—"

"He was a pathological liar. A disease or something."

"Some of that, at least *some* of that was a choice. What he did affected him, sure. But look how it's affected you. That makes me angry."

"Get over it." Deena stifled a snicker.

"I will if you will."

The café owner refilled their water glasses and asked if they needed boxes for their leftovers. In unison, the two women said, "Still working on it."

After the owner disappeared, they let the irony erupt in laughter. "Nice one, Pam."

"You, too. I guess we both have work to do."

The people Deena was supposed to trust taught her a language of lies and uncertainty. She couldn't be sure what they said, repeated, wrote, or claimed was true.

The boy she dated in high school said he loved her. That, too, was untrue. The words were a key he used to unlock what she'd intended to save for marriage. His lie netted her shame she can't shake. Her dad told her he loved her, too. The lies associated with those three little words taint them, even when they're spoken by her husband, a faithful, truth-telling man.

"Why do you flinch when I tell you I love you? Don't you believe me?"

"I *want* to."

Silence always follows the interchange.

Three years into their marriage, she's inching toward trust. But where trust is broken, even in childhood, the breach leaks toxic waste, plastering a thick coat of emotional sludge that often takes years and an enormous investment to clean up.

The greatest tragedy occurs when cleanup isn't addressed.

What would have happened if the Exxon or BP oil spills affecting the United States within the last decades didn't trigger a massive recovery effort? Yes, some of the damage would have dissipated in time, like residual effects of broken trust. But shorelines might still bear the gummy residue and the skeletons of oil-slicked wildlife if not for the cleanup efforts.

As part of her recovery, Deena peeled back the layers to one immutable truth: perfect, flawless trustworthiness is found in God alone. The most faithful, the most diligent among us remain capable of making errors in judgment, of forgetting, of failing those we love. Would her husband ever stumble with his words? Yes. Would he disappoint her? Yes. Was he committed to being as truthful with her as a human can? Yes.

Faith hinges on the wonder that God does not lie (Titus 1:2).

If only the rest of us would assume that as our default setting.

Deena described the truth as a foreign language about which she knew only a few basic words. What helped her progress past that state was her determination to learn more of the *language* of truth. She surrounded herself with trustworthy people, leaned on a trustworthy God, and fought off the natural inclination to assume everyone was as dishonest as those in her childhood and teen years had been.

Did she get stung again? A couple of times. And progress hasn't come easily.

But disillusionment is giving way to trust.

Reflections:

1. Whose untrustworthy words or actions had the strongest impact on you? Has trust been restored? How long or short a process has it been? What started you on the path toward restoration?

2. When it comes to trusting that God and the Bible are true, how much of your response depends on your circumstances? Describe the difference between "blind" faith and faith-with-good-reason.

3. Has your past created a habit of distrust in you? Can people trust your word?

If you know a *Deena* . . .

It's easy to grow annoyed with a person who battles trust issues. But if you've lived with or near a pathological liar or those who lie for their own gain, your empathy for the distrusting expands.

We prove ourselves trustworthy by being trustworthy. A series of trustworthy words and actions linked together form a dependability people like Deena crave.

Like Deena? We *all* crave dependability.

Mending trust isn't as simple as taping the broken ends together. Give your *Deena* time and space as you start back at the beginning, with the foundation: everything God does is worthy of our trust.

—————

All God's rules are trustworthy—
they are established always and forever:
they are fulfilled with truth and right doing.

PSALM 111:7-8

14. Stop Saying Grace

Tamara

WITH ONE SLICK MOVE, GARTH DREW THE YOUNG woman into his embrace and gained what he thought he wanted—someone who would listen to him without judging, a woman who met his every need.

That decision crashed a church, a family, and his marriage.

Like dominoes, other relationships fell when touched by Garth's choice to give in to the temptation of an affair. If he hadn't been the pastor, the wake he left might have dissipated before it reached shore. But he was the community's spiritual leader. The speedboat of his moral failure—aka *sin*—resulted in several capsizes and eventual drownings.

Garth's wife, Tamara, clung to the straps of her life preserver as she watched the waves lap over her sinking marriage. Titaniclike, it broke in two, the part above water offering a frail hope for a few too-brief moments. As she watched, it plummeted to a place even search teams couldn't find.

For a while, Tamara tanked, spiritually. Garth was her husband. "But he wasn't just *a* pastor; he was *my* pastor. The leader in our home. A connecting point in my relationship with the Lord and with our church. It was a community tragedy, but I was at the epicenter."

Families left the church. Some, disenchanted, didn't plug into another.

Propriety and denominational rulings stripped him of his pastorate, which meant the roles Tamara held since college graduation—pastor's wife and women's ministry leader—ended with his sin.

Garth moved out of the church-owned parsonage the week after he was found out. The church board gave Tamara and the kids a month to find a new home. The deadline was reduced to two weeks when the board found an interim pastor sooner than expected.

Everyone, including the pharmacist and the bag boy at the grocery store, looked at Tamara with an awkward pity and no words. No words.

Those who did talk shouldn't have.

"If a man gets what he needs at home . . ."

"I thought there might be trouble when Tamara started taking those speaking engagements."

"When a marriage breaks up, it's never just one person's fault, you know."

Yes. Sometimes it is.

And fault isn't the issue anyway. Fallout is.

Tamara lost everything, including the hope of reconciliation. Garth exhibited no remorse, refused counseling, and too-eagerly traded his wife and children for a new life with his lover and their baby on the way.

With Garth's termination, Tamara's and the kids' health insurance ended. Child support would have been nice. It arrived too spotty to count on—disrobed ministers aren't a hot hiring choice—and too sparse to make a difference.

The fractured family moved in with Tamara's parents until that relationship soured with unexpected accusations and mismatched goals—her parents bent on unearthing why Tamara hadn't seen it coming and why she now couldn't keep her teenage son from acting out.

They moved to a mobile home park six blocks and several eras away from the two-story colonial parsonage. Tamara took a job in the school cafeteria and signed up for food stamps. She hadn't known what it would cost her in humiliation to present a piece of government-issued debit card in exchange for milk and eggs.

Garth's choices—a series of them—could have destroyed her. But they didn't, in part because a fire ignited in Tamara that refused to let him take any more from her than he already had.

Though still grieving the loss of her marriage and the dissolution of what she thought was a forever relationship, she eventually came to realize that he'd keep scoring virtual points if she remained miserable. His affair and its consequences for her and the children had dominated her life too long. She reclaimed her dignity, investing the kind of effort she once expended on regret maintenance.

The maintenance costs for regret upkeep can bankrupt a person's spirit. Someone told her, "You're stronger than that." She believed it. A friend—one of the few who stuck it out through the messiness—encouraged her to recognize what radiated from God's Word, that God thought she was worth loving.

Tamara's attitude shifted. Garth had claimed too much emotional territory. She'd take some of it back. She'd relied so heavily on his defining who she was. She'd crawled into the mold he poured. When he was gone, nothing about her life held its shape.

But it didn't have to stay that way. Among the few remaining friends who told her what she wanted to hear was one who told her the truth—that she had choices of her own to make, choices that would drive the hurt deeper or that would reshape her life.

At the dinner table one night, she announced to the kids that they would no longer say grace before a meal.

They would give thanks and *live* grace. A minor adjustment with major repercussions.

As she healed, Tamara found that Garth's social network posts about his newborn son didn't bring the hurt she might have expected. She would sit at the computer, looking at her ex-husband's profile page, half-aware she shouldn't torture herself by peeking—and then discovered it wasn't as painful as she'd envisioned.

The uncommon peace she felt was, simply, the aftermath of God's mercy. She basked in the blessing of scars healing over.

The lingering consequences of Garth's choices—showing themselves in small ways and large—still stung but were more bearable with an extra layer of grace, like a tooth extraction *with* anesthesia as opposed to without it.

The more grace she and the kids showed to a community unsure how to react, the more adept the community became. Her unflagging joy-in-spite-of-it-all helped them see her not as a victim but as a woman of strong faith, not as Garth's poor ex-wife, *bless her heart*, but as Tamara Larson, a woman whose super-hero cape was fashioned from ragged hope.

On the shelf in my upstairs closet is a love-softened baby quilt estimated to be a hundred years old. Some of the quilt blocks are frayed at the seams. The color is faded from its original, but more beautiful because of its subtle hues. The edges are worn. Ragged.

But, like hope, those signs of wear don't make it less valuable. If anything, it would claim a higher price, if not in dollars then certainly in heart attachment. The wear shows what it's been through, how many babies it's enveloped, how many years it's endured, how many toddlers have dragged it behind them on miniature adventures.

If we think hope needs to be pristine and unwrinkled to be of any use, we might be missing the point. Fabric doesn't get that soft without life's pummeling. Hope that's endured increases in value.

If the hope to which you're clinging is showing signs of wear, consider how much more precious it's become.

Reflections:

1. Tamara refused to set up a permanent dwelling in the emotional manure pit her husband created. For the sake of her sanity, her children, and her faith, she allowed her faith to help her reimagine life with joy as its center and her past pain out on the periphery.

   Does that word picture resonate with you? Or do you react with, "I wish I could!" Take another look at Matthew 19:26 before responding.

2. Have you been devastated by a less-than-helpful reaction from your family, friends, or church when someone else's choices made you the subject of gossip? How did you handle it? What were the results?

3. The Bible tells us that God is "intimately acquainted" with our grief (Psalm 31:7). Tamara and her children are still discovering new layers of meaning in those words. How can that reassurance have an impact on what you're currently facing?

If you know a *Tamara* . . .

God leaves no loopholes for adultery. No excuses. No justifiable reasons. If a Tamara you know lapses into self-loathing or self-blame, remind her (or him) of that truth. Gently. Few hearts are as susceptible to reinjury.

Do you know someone in church leadership who can identify with Tamara's story? How are you reaching out, past your own discomfort, to encourage those affected? What can you do before this day is over to show that your prayer support hasn't ended . . . and won't?

So they cried out to the LORD in their distress,
and God brought them out safe from
their desperate circumstances.

PSALM 107:28

15. My Sister's an Only Child

Maria

SHE STARED AT THE CARPET AT HER FEET. IT occupied a lot of her attention. Making eye contact wasn't high on her list of life goals. For a twentysomething, that promised a carpet-rich but friendless future.

I complimented her on the song she'd shared with our congregation that morning and expressed words I assumed would encourage her. "Your parents must be so pleased you're using your beautiful voice this way."

She looked up only briefly. "I wouldn't know. My sister is an only child."

The story unfolded slowly, as if each word caused her pain.

"When my mother married my stepfather, he let her know he couldn't love me. She married him anyway and asked me to move out. I was fifteen. They had my half-sister a few months later. In my mom's eyes, Theresa is an only child."

Could you have thought of a response more than, "I'm so sorry"?

Neither could I.

It might have been in response to the tears I cried for her, for a young woman whose parents discarded her as inconvenient to their plans, but her words tumbled out then like battered candy from a tortured piñata.

"Where did you live after they kicked you out?" I asked.

Carpet fibers. "Here and there. With friends. With people I thought were my friends."

"Did you finish high school?"

"Yeah. Most of my teachers didn't know I was homeless. I brushed my teeth in the girls' restroom. Changed clothes in one of the stalls. Signed my mom's name to permission slips. When I got mail, my mom would leave it in an old coffee can on the back porch. Once in a while I'd go past there to check."

My imagination wanted to believe the mother regretted her decision. "Did your mom leave notes? Money?"

Maria laughed but didn't look up. "Yeah, she left a note

once. 'Tell the post office to forward your mail to wherever it is you're staying.'"

I couldn't walk away as if I'd asked, "How ya doin'?" and she'd answered, "Fine."

"I hope you found a safe place to live, Maria."

She shifted the baby on her hip. "Still looking."

People are breakable. They should come stamped *Fragile*.

When Jesus said it, He put it this way: "Whoever welcomes one such child in my name welcomes me. As for whoever causes these little ones who believe in me to trip and fall into sin, it would be better for them to have a huge stone hung around their necks and be drowned in the bottom of the lake" (Matthew 18:5-6).

I first heard that verse with the term "millstone." As the broken child with a fatherless baby on her hip stood with me in what we call the *sanctuary*—for good reason—I considered how I could get my hands on a millstone.

But calling those pseudo-parents to task for what they'd done to this young woman didn't fall under jobs God appointed to me. God has His own exquisitely detailed plans for millstone parents, and those plans no doubt are laced with far more grace than I harbor.

If it takes eight positive touches to neutralize one negative word—I read that somewhere—then how much love, how much reassurance does it take to counteract the parental message, "You don't exist"?

I couldn't waste any time getting started trying.

But Maria had steeled herself against further injury, like a burn victim might flinch at a fireplace flame others find comforting.

And she wasn't alone. I heard a similar story from motherless young women two more times within weeks of meeting Maria. How is that possible?

God wondered the same thing. Can a mother forsake her child?

The prophet Isaiah asked, "Can a woman forget her nursing child, / fail to pity the child of her womb?" (Isaiah 49:15).

Harsh reality check: some moms do. The second half of that verse seems to ride on a divine sigh punctuated with a promise: "Even these may forget, / but I won't forget you."

The psalmist David identified with people like Maria when he wrote, "Even if my father and mother left me all alone, / the LORD would take me in" (Psalm 27:10).

Take me in. Sanctuary.

How long will it be before Maria and others like her risk embracing the life-affecting comfort, "But I won't forget you"?

And there's still the matter of the mother who should have known better.

It's come up in conversation too frequently in recent years. "What do you mean? She walked away from her kids? Just walked away? She got tired of being a mom? Freedom meant more to her than her babies? How is that possible?"

The stories are more complicated than that. And rarely one-sided. But it's hard to understand what could distance a mother's heart from her children. It's even harder to understand how the abandoned could bear the sight of a mother walking away.

We can try to couch it in words easier to swallow—*She isn't in her right mind. She had to follow her dreams. She needed some space*—but the reality for the abandoned or neglected reads this way: *She chose something or someone else above her love for me.*

An empathetic ache throbs in my stomach as I write this.

Is it enough for the abandoned to know that God would never forsake them?

It has to be enough. For their sakes, we pray, "Lord, please make it enough!"

Another chapter has been written in Maria's story. She married a tenderhearted man who cherishes her. Where others might use abandonment to make excuses for antisocial behavior and a rut of pain, Maria and her husband have cultivated a passion for international adoption. Maria turned her abandonment issues into adoption forms. The children she and her husband welcome into their home will know they are loved.

Reflections:

1. Are you living in the fallout, the aftermath of abandonment or neglect? Draw your chair closer. One of the most

important truths of Scripture was written for you. God said, "I will never leave you or abandon you" (Hebrews 13:5b).

The God who loved you before you were aware of His presence or His intentions to woo you promised that He would never leave you or forsake you. Meditate on that truth until it pierces through the walls built around your heart.

2. What does it do to your spirit when you note that God's promise never to give you up, never to let go of those He loves, is not merely mentioned in the Bible but repeated for emphasis? Read and reflect on passages like Genesis 28:15, Deuteronomy 31:6, and Joshua 1:5.

Even if you haven't experienced that kind of faithfulness from the people around you, you can lean your head back against the heartbeat of an ever-faithful God.

3. "If I can't make my mom choose me, I'll choose to be like her." The words may not be spoken aloud, the tendency recognized. But it is a pattern that often reaches the psychologist's ears. How have you resisted the pull to hurt others the way you've been hurt? Where do you draw the strength to love like you wish you'd been loved?

If you know a *Maria* . . .

Sometimes counselors recommend news-fast therapy—turning off the news in order to lessen stress. Our hearts twist when we hear reports—almost daily, it seems—of children abandoned, abused, neglected. Children held captive in basement dungeons by senseless parents who starve them both physically and emotionally. Children whose x-rays are road maps of abuse. Children drained of the joy and exuberance that their age should have made hard to contain. Children robbed of hope.

Will you join me in praying right now for mercy for the children of millstone parents?

Will you also join me in watching for ways to point those children to resources for help? Can your church community or small group become a tangible answer when an abandoned young person needs a place to stay and an example of what real love looks like? How well-informed are you about the services available and the steps you can take to get personally involved?

———

He will never leave his faithful all alone.
They are guarded forever.
PSALM 37:28

16. She Loved to Dance

Cherise

I'D INTENDED IT TO BE A REMINDER ABOUT THE fragility of life.

During a mother/daughter tea, my talk included the story of my granddaughter's field trip a week earlier. When parent and grandparent chaperones like me walked through the school's double doors, we were greeted by the school counselor who ushered us into an empty classroom across the hall from the one in which the third-graders waited. I expected a list of instructions—which prankster to watch for, how to successfully defuse a meltdown, the location of the car sickness buckets on the school bus . . .

Instead, with the children's voices across the hall registering their excitement about the day's upcoming adventure at the state capital, a teacher and the counselor told us why we'd been separated from the children. One of the students' classmates had died in the night—a ten-year-old girl who'd taught her young friends the meaning of the word *oncology*.

We had a corporate decision to make. Should we cancel the field trip or continue with the intricately orchestrated plans? In that suddenly somber room, those of us more distant from the immediate scene deferred to those closest to the little girl and her best friends. The classroom knew she'd grown weaker during the past weeks. They'd written another batch of encouragement cards and prepared their hearts, as best as children—or any of us—can for the day when her body would be too weak to carry on.

With the approval of the counselor who believed the class needed to be together, needed one another, and needed a cadre of parents and grandparents willing to dry tears and listen to broken hearts, the decision was made to go forward with the plans. As soon as we broke the news to the students.

We adults filed into the room across the hall and found the student or students dearest to us. The teachers handled the announcement with grace and a compassion that added to the tender tears. We grieved briefly, knowing it was Phase One of a many-phased sorrow. None were unaffected. Then we wiped our tears, climbed on the bus, and leaned on one another as we started toward the capital two hours away.

The resilience of the young showed itself in the way the students deeply felt the loss of their classmate, then relearned how to laugh before a hundred highway hash marks flew by.

As I shared the story with the mothers and daughters at the tea that next week, I knew I risked inserting sadness into an event that was billed as a celebration. But I'd been affected by the reminder that any of us can cross the line between here and eternity before the day's end. The things we fret about lose their battery power in light of that indisputable reality.

At the conclusion of the event, a young girl stood among others in line to talk to me. Thirteen or fourteen years old and visibly uncomfortable, she waited at the end of the line, fidgeting as if eager to talk but not in front of others.

When I was free to ask what was on her heart, Cherise told me she'd lost a classmate, too. Five years earlier, her friend stayed overnight with her after dance class. In the morning, Cherise and her mom took the little girl, Allie, home. Within an hour, Allie was dead.

The evening news broke the story and a townful of hearts. In a fit of unexplained fury, Allie's father took a gun to his wife, his daughter, and himself.

I'd spoken for over an hour and was now speechless. Every word my mind tested, it discarded as grossly inadequate for Cherise's pain. I settled for, "Oh, honey," and a hug.

The unsaid hovered invisibly in the room. What if they'd

delayed taking her home? Would that have changed the out-come? Why should one so young have to wrestle those kinds of questions?

As I held Cherise and heard the rest of her story, I was con-scious of the fallout of Allie's father's insanity, ashes that fell on the shoulders of the person opening her heart to me.

"Five years ago," I said, my insides cramping with the remnants of how that tragedy must have affected the then eight-year-old. "What now, Cherise?"

She smiled.

"How do you cope?" It wasn't a challenge question. I saw uncommon, well-practiced wisdom in her eyes and wanted to coax it into the open.

Her smile broadened. "I keep dancing. Allie loved to dance. I keep dancing for her."

Resilience. Cherise could teach resilience classes. And grief classes—how to honor someone's memory in a way that pre-serves the beauty of life rather than the ugliness that took it.

It's as if Cherise's body movements communicate, "I dance so others know they can keep dancing even when life gets hard." How did she get so wise?

Even today, more than a year after hearing her story, I'm impressed she'd grasped such a soul-revitalizing concept so young. She discovered a positive way to honor her friend and grieve her loss. With each dance move, she strengthened the muscles of her faith.

I wish I could have told Cherise that was the only trauma

she'd ever face. It might rate as the most dramatic, but it wouldn't be the last.

Sometimes when the actions of other people steal our breath, our friends, our joy, all we can do is keep dancing. And the dance itself forms a graceful rhythm for others to adopt as their own.

Reflections:

1. How elastic is your heart? How quickly does it rebound from crimes committed against it?
2. What keeps the human heart pliable? What hardens it, makes it brittle?
3. The tentative first steps of someone learning to dance may seem awkward, clumsy. God sees them as elegant because to dance at all when life is hard is an accomplishment. In what ways are you a well-practiced dancer?

If you know a *Cherise* . . .

How many young people struggle to find an adult willing to listen to their story, no matter how long it takes to tell?

Are you willing to listen and listen some more so you're present when a broken-winged little one confesses why his or her life hasn't been the same since that day when . . . ?

God heals the brokenhearted
and bandages their wounds.
PSALM 147:3

17. Out in the Cold

Dave

SHIRTSLEEVES IN MIDWINTER. IN THE NORTH woods. What's wrong with this picture?

We didn't know the whole story when we first met Dave, but we knew something other than "I never wear a coat" stood behind his reasoning. It was years into our relationship with him before my husband and I heard the truth.

Dave worshiped with us, attended several recovery support groups, and offered the blessing of his presence and a unique, faith-stretching perspective to our Bible study. Faith came alive in fresh ways as we watched him discover a God who loved him intensely yet tenderly. I remember the tears that spilled when he confessed, "I'm learning to let God *father* me."

Dave's father had made it his life's ambition to humiliate Dave in every way possible. All his creative forces bore down on shaming his son. Growing up in that degrading atmosphere set the course for many of Dave's life choices.

Shame served as his engraved-in-the-flesh-of-his-heart invitation to a laundry list of addictions. Shame sullied every relationship. Shame forced him into seclusion.

Dave's choices, yes. But his choices were forged on the anvil of his father's relentless humiliation.

In the safe acceptance of our small group study, Dave shared tiny shards of his history and his real self, as if testing to see if we would react as his father did. We didn't balk. So he shared more.

One night, he told us the story behind his coatlessness.

A young boy at the time, he'd gone to the movies with friends, but had forgotten his jacket at the theater.

"Where's your coat?" his father demanded. He must have forgotten to say, "Hi. Glad you're home safe. Did you have a good time?"

When Dave told him what happened, the tirade started. "Irresponsible idiot! You have a brain don't you? Don't you? Try using it sometime. What kind of idiot leaves his coat at the movies?"

"I'll go back tomorrow and get it, Dad."

"You're not worth the trouble. Freeze to death for all I care. You know what? That's a good idea. Teach you a lesson. A coat's no big deal? Try sleeping outside without it tonight. Front lawn. In front of everybody. 'See me? I'm the idiot who left his coat at the movies.'"

"Dad!"

"You think I'm kidding? You're stupider than I thought."

Every sentence was punctuated with the makings of a new fist-shaped bruise.

His father's disapproving glare and belittling barbs for Dave's "unforgiveable" neglect and other equally despicable misdeeds gained momentum that wouldn't let up until the casket lid closed over the dad's unseeing eighty-year-old eyes decades later.

When Dave was a child, enduring the chill of a shaming father and a coatless night huddled at the base of a tree in the front yard, he determined it would never happen again.

He couldn't forget his jacket if he didn't wear one.

Forty years later, he still braved frigid temperatures without a coat.

The sting of a parent's rebuke lingers, its icy fingers colder than winter.

Week after week at our Bible study group, Dave heard about God—a different kind of Father, one who embraces those who shiver, who wraps His arms around those who forget things, who draws errant children to His chest and soothes them with the steady rhythm of His heartbeat.

I wonder if angels danced as much as we did the night Dave came to church wearing a fleece-lined coat.

The classic breakup line is, "It's not you. It's me." Rarely convincing.

A healing step in coping with the aftereffects from those intent on shaming us turns that line inside out. "It's not me. It's you. It really is you."

A pattern of destructive shaming is a sign of a malfunctioning heart or mind or both. Dave's eyes widened when he recognized that the root of the shame wasn't his behavior but his dad's dysfunction. "It was *his* problem. Not mine."

The thought took root slowly. More like an avocado pit than an African violet slip. But it grew.

Dave had been a perfect attendance student at the school of shame. He had a lot of unlearning to do.

At a recent small group meeting, Dave was asked, "What would you say to someone suffocating under that kind of abuse?"

"If the shame fits, wear it? Joke. That was a joke."

We waited while he allowed himself to get serious, to see his father's tactics for the abuse they were.

"I'd say shaming isn't the same thing as parenting. I'd say take responsibility for your actions, but don't let anyone substitute humiliation for a relationship."

One hurdle conquered. Around the room, pens scrambled to jot down his words.

(Author's note: Now that he's wearing one, Dave's never forgotten his coat.)

Reflections:

1. How have harsh words changed or formed a pattern in your life? How have they affected the way you view your faith connection with God?

2. Have you relinquished your hold on unforgiveness? Since forgiveness is a process—with a beginning, a middle, and an end—where are you in that process? What moves you forward? How does a passage like Psalm 139:23-24 feed your courage as you learn to forgive the undeserving?

3. Consider watching for Scripture verses and evidence around you that reveal God's protective nature. You may already know people in your circle of friends and family who need to hear their restorative whispers, too.

If you know a *Dave* . . .

Behind every quirk, every oddity, every curiosity is a story. But those stories are hiding until they know it's safe to walk out into the open without fear of ridicule or condemnation.

It takes a lot of love to un-humiliate someone, to neutralize caustic words, to help repair broken confidence. Love and time. God is invested in the process.

I have to ask myself if I'm as invested, or if I'm quicker to add to the shame rather than listen for its root.

God will protect you with his pinions;
you'll find refuge under his wings.
His faithfulness is a protective shield.

PSALM 91:4

18. Laid to Rest

Jeremiah

EIGHTY YEARS AFTER THE FACT, HE STILL COULDN'T talk about it. His sister Lizabeth had preceded him in death by eight decades. Now on his own deathbed, he still couldn't bring himself to talk about her or forgive his father.

When horses and buggies outnumbered automobiles on the country roads in the farmlands of middle America, Jeremiah worked his father's fields and tended the animals with a devotion beyond his sixteen years. He picked rocks, plowed, and planted. He fed hogs and calves, milked cows, put up hay, gathered eggs, fed the chickens, butchered meat and poultry for the table, working alongside his sullen father. Often he worked in place of his father, whose infatuation with strong drink troubled Jeremiah's mom, frustrated Jeremiah, and frightened his fourteen-year-old sister, Lizabeth.

His father's drinking sprees fueled a wicked temper that erupted in abusive language and irrational behavior. Jeremiah's respect for his father shriveled. It died altogether the day Lizabeth died.

Jeremiah was working a field on the ridge when he saw a cloud of dust trailing behind a racing jenny-rig. His dad had gone into town with Lizabeth. By the speed of the rig, Jeremiah could guess what occupied his time and attention in town.

He stopped working and watched as the rig neared the bridge at the bottom of the valley. Watched as the lathered horse clattered onto the narrow wooden structure. Watched as the right wheels of the rig slipped under the railing and the buggy flipped on its side and plunged into the creek, dragging the horse after it.

Jeremiah's shouts slid down the hill with him. He hurdled the fence and the ditch and waded to his waist in the creek water. Lizabeth was pinned under the rig, face-first in the water. Lifeless. Such an inelegant death, with horse hooves thrashing and the smell of alcohol thick on his irresponsible, groaning father.

The boy carried his sister's body to the farmhouse, then put the horse out of its misery and his father out of his mind. Forever.

Years later, Jeremiah's grandchildren worked on family tree projects for school and asked their beloved grandfather about their ancestry. He refused to fill in the blank representing his father, refused to talk about him, or allow any other relative to talk about him.

A gentle man in every other way, he was a block of cold granite on the topic of his father. To date, little is known about his father and the curious rumors tracing back yet another generation.

Crippled emotionally by his father's reckless choices, Jeremiah went to his grave without finding peace on that topic. What should have been sweet memories of a much-loved sister were marred by the way she died and the man who caused her death.

And we, *Jeremiah's* grandchildren, will never know the whole story of our great-grandfather.

The fallout of my great-grandfather's choices choked off part of our family tree, leaving gaps in our family history, unanswered questions, and a relentless curiosity about what fueled my great-grandfather's desperation. What fallout was he laboring under? How far back in time lay the genesis of the cycle of pain?

My grandfather was a dear, hardworking, fun-loving man. But a shadow would cross his face at unexpected moments.

We knew he was thinking of *Lizabeth* and trying hard not to think about the man whose name he refused to utter.

It's hard for me to reconcile my gentle grandfather with his harsh silence about his father. As full a life as he lived, well into his nineties, we all sensed that he forever saw himself as a sixteen-year-old boy with his sister's limp body in his arms, carrying her up the hill, his father's slurred, garbled cries for help at his back.

The decisions we make in the fallout of other people's choices can lead us out of the fog or drive us deeper into it, where nobody wins.

We have the yellowed newspaper account of the event that took Lizabeth's life. We don't have Grandpa to ask about the rest of the story.

How can any of us know how we would react under the same circumstances? I'd like to think I'd value the freedom of forgiveness more than my brokenness over my loss. I'd like to believe I could learn to live without the shadows. Even though my grandfather has been gone many years, I ache for the gap his pain kept blank on our family tree.

Reflections:

1. Only God knows the whole truth about those men on our family tree. Only God knows what might have transpired in my grandfather's heart regarding forgiveness or acceptance. Maybe his pain eased as he neared heaven's gates.

Who in your circle of family or friends seems perpetually saddened by an incident from the past? Is it you?

2. In what ways have you seen generational fallout affect your family?

3. I didn't know my great-grandfather at all. But I deeply loved my grandpa. In some ways, that means without realizing it, I, too, hold the thought of my great-grandfather at an uncomfortable distance. I don't know the whole story, but I know my great-grandfather caused my grandfather inexplicable pain. A court of law would call that hearsay. I've formed an opinion based on someone else's opinion. Not until now did I realize that I need to forgive him, and I don't even know the extent of all he did. If a name from your family tree came to mind just now, are you ready to lay to rest any pain that person caused?

If you know a *Jeremiah* . . .

You might be more successful than our family at coaxing out the stories. If Grandpa could have talked about it, would it have given him a sense of release? We can't know. There may be someone in your family who is hurting, longing for someone to care enough to ask where the pain originated. Someone who won't flinch when the person starts talking, raw and ragged as the story might be.

The Jeremiah in this chapter represents thousands of people like him who carry around a deeply impacting private pain. They may never be ready to talk. But we can stand ready to listen if they do and pray for a bright hope to over-shadow their distress.

I pour out my concerns before God;
I announce my distress to him.
When my spirit is weak inside me,
you still know my way.

PSALM 142:2-3

19. Not a Whisper of Regret

Jayne

JAYNE SUSPECTED HER HUSBAND, KYLE, OF HAVING an affair. His secrecy. His refusal to answer his cell phone. His inability to look her in the eye over the dinner table the rare nights he was home.

Other behaviors didn't fit the pattern, if she could believe any number of television dramas and tragic love stories. He'd sold his motorcycle, claiming he was getting ready for retirement, even though his bike had figured heavily into Kyle's retirement plans. He'd seemed almost hostile when their son and daughter-in-law asked for a donation to the kidney fund drive for a fellow teacher. Nothing fit Kyle's norm as she'd known it for the forty years they'd been married.

And faithful to one another.

When the phone rang on a Tuesday morning, a wave of dread swept over her. Other than the churning in her stomach, she had no reason to believe the call was ominous. But her hand trembled as she reached for the receiver.

"Jayne, it's Rob Bennett. Look, I know Kyle's under the weather again—bummer about the chemo—and I wouldn't disturb him but he's the only one with the passcode for last year's internal audit notes. The corporate board is meeting, and they're asking for those figures. I hate to do this to him, but do you think he's up to talking to me for a sec?"

Under the weather. Again. Chemo. Up to talking.

"He doesn't . . . he's not . . ."

"Like I said, I hated to call. Have him text me, okay? He doesn't have to talk."

"I'll . . . I'll find out for you." *Just as soon as I find out where he is.*

Kyle didn't answer his cell phone. Nothing new there. She redialed. No answer. She left a message, then texted him that work had called with an urgent need. Wherever he was, he wasn't where he was supposed to be.

Within an hour, he was home. Jayne calculated how many sleazy hotels were within an hour's drive. Too many.

"You're looking good," she said, arms crossed, "considering how devastating the chemo treatments have been." The vinegar in her voice made her throat constrict.

"Jayne," he set his useless briefcase on the floor, "we have to talk."

"Who is she?"

"She?"

"Kyle, you're in too deep to lie to me now." Jayne leaned against the outer edge of the arm of her wing chair. She couldn't imagine sitting down for this.

In the end, the wing chair was one of the many things sold at the garage sale. No longer a place to lean, to read, to dream, it paid for groceries the week of Kyle's indictment for embezzlement.

Before his confession, Jayne pictured her husband locked in a disturbingly passionate embrace with a woman he met on the Internet, their rendezvous a pathetic place with a name like "Don't Tell Motel" and "Shh!" as its marketing tagline.

But he'd been having an affair with a roulette wheel, losing their mortgage payment, their savings, and their dignity.

He'd had no choice, he said, but to *borrow* from work. Wisely, his court-appointed lawyer advised against putting him on the stand during his trial.

The gambling addiction support group met in a community center across town. Kyle didn't think they could afford the gas money. They needed it for legal fees.

The move from their suburban ranch home to a slumped apartment building with unnaturally wavy vinyl siding took place during a downpour and an important meeting with his lawyer. If circumstances had been different, the guys from work would have been the logical choice to help with the move. Jayne didn't know anyone well enough yet at the convenience store where she'd gotten a job. Two young men—their son's friends from church—showed up but said, "Hey, don't tell my mom I'm here, okay?"

"I'm not the criminal!" she cried deep in her chest. But she bore the overspray of a criminal's shame.

At Kyle's sentencing, she had an opportunity to speak a word on his behalf. She couldn't think of anything to say.

The guards dragged him off to a minimum security prison. She dragged herself home.

"Is he gone?" her son asked.

"Yes."

"Good."

Nothing about their lives seemed familiar or survivable, including the emotional disconnects.

The calendar now marked more than birthdays and doctor appointments. All other activities adjusted themselves around visitation day, which Jayne attended alone. She picked at the hole in her jeans as she listened to Kyle's remorseless designs for his loophole appeal.

Six months, she listened for a whisper of remorse.

On the seventh-month's visit, she announced she wasn't draining her retirement fund to pay for an appeal. He'd need to work on his "good behavior" chances. She had to adjust the rearview mirror on the drive home that day. Higher. She was sitting taller.

Her thinking shifted as dramatically. She couldn't affect his imprisonment, but she could affect hers. Her sympathy for his incarceration and his loss of freedom remained. Her love for him held on by a ragged, tenacious thread. But where she'd ignored her own needs previously, she began to plug holes through which her spirit leaked out.

Although the fallout of his choices was noisy, clattering, reverberating through every aspect of life, she worked on recreating a scene she could live with. Kyle had stolen so much, including hope. It was time to reclaim it.

Emotionally, she couldn't afford to wait until he felt the impact of what he'd done to their family. That date might never come, despite her prayers. Time to regroup, to marshal her energies to do more than just survive.

Changing her husband's mind-set was beyond her abilities. Only the One who made him could change him.

For Jayne, establishing new routines felt as traumatic at first as the middle-aged woman who hadn't cut her long mane of hair since junior high but submitted to a makeover that started with very big scissors. The weight of the hair fell away to the accompaniment of a flood of bright tears.

Jayne held the "ponytail" of her former dreams in her hand and made the decision to donate it all to the equivalent of "Locks of Love."

"Where do people like me go to find a safe place to talk about how my husband's bad decisions changed my life, not just his? Who do I talk to who won't think less of my husband when I moan about discovering one more hidden debt, one more humiliation, one more consequence I'm now responsible to bear?"

Her instincts told her she couldn't be the only woman in the world who loved a man who'd made lousy choices but was still a man worth loving. She considered forming a group called "Never Gonna Leave Him, But I Don't Have to Like Him." Deleted that idea.

Eventually, with the guidance of the pastoral staff from her church, she established a branch of ministry adopted from a similar group in a neighboring town. The women met weekly to maintain their sanity while coping with wounds slow to heal. They tackled topics such as how to keep resentment from escalating to an explosive state, how to view their spouse as a leader even when the decision-making defaulted to the unimprisoned one, and where to find reliable financial advice for uprighting what had been upended.

Jayne's "Locks of Love" equivalent meant finding a way, some way, any way to reclaim life from what had been cut off. Using her pain to bless someone else lent it a dignity it didn't have naturally. Restorative recycling.

The secrecy and deception of Kyle's addiction that led to sin that led to a prosecutable crime carried a soul-deep sting that in some ways smarted more than the endless wave of consequences from his actions. If he'd expressed remorse, forgiveness would have come far more easily.

She forgave . . . for her own sake, because unforgiveness wouldn't help either of them. He made it harder by not admitting his guilt and not recognizing how his actions affected every corner of life. She forgave anyway.

Before he was caught, Jayne hadn't thought about gambling as an addiction. An obsession, maybe. If it had started as that, it too quickly became full-blown addiction for Kyle, the kind that threw his moral compass into a frenzied spin and fed him lies that justified his actions. If he'd let her into that part of his life and his struggle when it was young, she might have been able to steer him toward the help he needed before he slid into the slick-walled pit.

She wasn't allowed that option—to offer or direct him toward help. That frustration became another layer of fallout.

Jayne's story isn't included here to show one more incident of financial reversal or one more marriage in trouble or one more kind of addiction and its consequences.

I told her story because I admire Jayne's stamina and the way she learned how to step up and take charge when she wasn't used to that role. She courageously made a decision to do the right thing rather than what her delusional husband wanted. And that started her climb out from under the ash heap of what he'd done to their lives. I admire the way she started her own reclamation project—turning her experience into something useful for others.

Has her husband come to his senses yet? I haven't heard.

But I imagine heaven is as proud of her as I am for not waiting until he asked before she forgave him.

Reflections:

1. From what well do you draw the strength to forgive when the offender doesn't seem sorry?
2. What circumstance in your life could benefit from a "Locks of Love" approach—recycling the pain to bless others? How have you turned the thought into action?
3. Do you journal? What role does journaling play when people disappoint or devastate you?

If you know a *Jayne* . . .

In what ways can you show your *Jayne* that you know her husband's bad choices were his, not hers? It's natural to keep our distance from those whose story is painful. How can you ensure she doesn't feel abandoned, branded, or labeled? Do you have a strong enough relationship with her that you sense when she needs to talk about it and when she needs to talk about anything except the fallout? Do you have a strong enough relationship with God that He can whisper His guidance to you in that regard?

*I have remained faithful, even when I said,
"I am suffering so badly!"*
PSALM 116:10

20. Untouchable Scars

Marissa

"IT'S A GIRL! CONGRATULATIONS!"

Steve assumed his wife's tears registered the kind of euphoria he felt. Their first child. Born beautiful, without the traditional waiting for the head bumps of its travels through the birth canal to recede.

"What do you think about Annalise?" he asked Marissa, confirming their top choice for a baby girl's name.

Marissa nodded and swiped at her tears but turned her face away from the child now resting on her chest.

"I was hoping for a boy," she said when days later her doctor joined Steve in questioning her lack of attachment to her newborn daughter. The next day, Marissa's smile returned, though Steve's peripheral vision caught its quick fade when he turned his attention from her face.

Postpartum depression dogged the family that first year. Annalise charmed everyone but her mother, who seemed unable to do more than tolerate the child who blessedly slept through the night and entertained herself.

Despite Steve's misgivings, Marissa wanted to become pregnant—and did—before Annalise's first birthday. The pregnancy evened something in Marissa's mood. Her smile seemed less plastic, more genuine. Joy crept back into what had been mechanical mothering. She still left much of the hands-on care of their daughter to Steve, but Marissa seemed more connected.

Marissa painted the nursery alcove blue, bought blue blankets, and packed a blue sleeper for bringing the new baby home.

It was a girl.

Annalise and her infant sister, Lara, lived with their father when Marissa checked herself into a mental health facility the day she and the new baby should have been discharged from the hospital. It was eight weeks and several failed medications into treatment before the psychologists coaxed the truth from her, a truth she hadn't told Steve because she didn't realize it existed.

She had a deep-rooted fear of raising daughters.

Irrational as it seemed, somewhere in her subconscious lurked a fear that she could not protect a little girl, that she would make the kind of twisted choice her mother made in Marissa's childhood. She couldn't risk that.

Her mother had loved her. No question. But love wasn't enough to shield Marissa from the abuse that took place almost every night after her mother's boyfriend moved in. Her mother knew. She had to have known. The bruises, the stains, the night terrors, the tears. Marissa's mother would hold her daughter's face, her thumbs gently tracing the line of recent bruises, then turn and walk away.

Marissa would never walk away from a daughter's cries for help. She would give birth to boys only. And she would teach them how not to crush a child.

Annalise's birth had dragged a primal scream from the depths of Marissa's experience. A girl? No! Not a girl!

Her mind couldn't process having *another* daughter. Wound tight inside, she'd pulled herself together enough to survive and to offer the appearance—to all but Steve—that everything was okay. But with the birth of a second daughter, the wheels came off.

Knowing the truth about why she derailed didn't bring instant healing. It rarely does. It offered an explanation for her irrational disconnect from her children. But it was another two years of therapy, unconditional love, and gut-wrenching prayer before Marissa's scars healed enough to be touched. There was a reason for her fear. And there was a Healer who cared. Her therapist helped her uncover the reason. Her Healer God uncovered a long-buried hope.

She'd missed the crucial early years of bonding with her then toddler daughters. Determined to make up for the attachment she and they missed, Marissa struggled for balance. Detachment and smothering sat on either end of the teeter-totter of her life, and they rarely held a perfect horizontal.

Marissa's mother's sin of omission—of not intervening, not telling, ignoring the abuse—formed a toxic, acidic cloud that permeated Marissa's soul.

Marissa made a single choice that walked her and their family toward healing. She sought help. She opted for a new kind of "labor" in order to give birth to a healthier understanding of who she was as a woman and parent.

Marissa was not like her mother. She was more aware, alert, and well-prepared than her mother had been, trained in part by her own crippling experiences and by the counselors who in some ways served as personal trainers to help strengthen the muscles of her resolve.

And she'd married a man the polar opposite of her abuser. She leaned into his stability and drew courage for her own.

In time, she braved reaching out to other victims of abuse, using her own story to encourage others living with the aftermath of abuse. Supported by her husband and counselors, Marissa determined to allow God to do in her what He'd done for the Old Testament Joseph and others—turning what was meant for evil into something God could use for good.

Genesis 50:20 records Joseph's response to the family members who treated him with unconscionable cruelty and then abandoned him to his pain. "You planned something bad for me, but God produced something good from it, in order to save the lives of many people, just as he's doing today."

Joseph forgave his brothers before they asked.

When Marissa's mother broke her vow of silence with a simple "I'm sorry," Marissa was ready with a response.

"I forgive you."

"I was afraid that if I—"

"No, Mom. No excuses. No explanations. Not yet. Just know I forgive you."

Like a scarred, battered hardwood floor in the process of restoration, her healing still needs refining, polishing, another protective layer applied. But the hope once buried in fallout ashes is now exposed to the light.

Those who work with victims of sexual abuse struggle with their own fallout issues. Brokenhearted over the ruined lives they encounter every day, they battle depression, anger, hopelessness, a choking cloud of despair over the atrocities borne by the victims.

Trace with me the path of pain in a case like Marissa's. Who was affected by the fallout? Marissa. Her mother.

Marissa's children and husband. Anyone who cared about her. Her counselors and pastor and church friends and . . . and now, you.

Some of us can close the covers of this book and set her story aside. Some will relive the aftermath of their own stories, their path of pain generations long, the consequences radically more severe.

Marissa's story could have ended with the same chain of silence and intolerable pain her mother's household held or even worse tragedy. It might have, if she hadn't reached out for professional help, and if she hadn't believed she could trust a God whose heart broke with hers.

Reflections:

1. We are framed and shaped by our past, among other things. But some of us try to make forward progress while we're facing—consumed by—our unchangeable past. Imagine walking backward through life. How easy is it to get tripped up that way? In what sense have you been walking backward as you strive to move forward? Are you moving at all?

2. Where do the shadows lie when we have our backs to the sun? In front of us. And the shadows are behind us when we face the light source. How does that principle show itself true in your life when you consider God as your source of light?

3. People with deep, excruciating pain in their personal history can't erase the past. But they can keep it to their backs—the shadows present but not affecting forward progress—when they change positions and turn their faces toward the light. Is it time to position yourself spiritually so the shadows remain behind you and you can more confidently move into your future? Have you reached out for help?

If you know a *Marissa* . . .

Just as Job's friends from the Bible served a greater purpose when they simply sat with him rather than trying to explain his distress, search for reasons, and affix blame, your greatest gift to your friend or family member will likely be your presence.

The reverberations of an adult's betrayal and a parent's failure to protect a child resonate far into the future. Human words rarely interrupt those sound waves. But a human presence can. And a Divine Presence can rewrite the end of the story. If you know a *Marissa*, make sure she knows where help can be found . . . and that you care.

Hope in God!
Because I will again give him thanks,
my saving presence and my God.
PSALM 43:5

21. Dream Changer

Trey

"OOH! FOR ME?" VICKI DROPPED HER GARDENING gloves and clapped her hands together. "What's in the box?"

Trey bumped the driver's door shut with his hip. "My life."

Vicki edged closer. "Come on. Let me see. What's really in there?" She tugged on the sleeve of his suit jacket. "Oh, you sweet man! Did you get me that Teddy Bear puppy I had my eye on at the shelter? Trey, you're amazing. I love you so—"

He cut her off with an unreadable blank look and a shrug of his shoulder.

"Trey?"

Stopping short of the back entrance to their home, he set the box on the ground and turned to face her. "Sorry. I should have called right away. But I didn't know what to say."

"What's wrong?"

"I'm officially a statistic."

She tilted her head as if it would help her understand his ramblings.

"I wear a scarlet U on my chest."

"What?"

"I'm now among the Unemployed." Trey's eyes widened, jaw tight.

"I don't understand. You're two months from retirement. That's impossible. They can't let you go when you're—"

"Can and did."

"Isn't that illegal?"

"Unethical. Unkind. But apparently not illegal in this state. They're calling it 'regrettable but necessary resizing.' Aren't even calling it downsizing anymore."

Vicki curled into his embrace as she had for thirty-five years of marriage. "So, you were forced to retire a little early. It'll be okay."

He pulled away from her optimism. "You're not listening."

"Hey, I'm not the enemy here."

Trey apologized with his eyes, then drew her back into his arms. "It's not going to be okay, Vicki. This isn't early retirement."

He let her go and lowered himself to the cement stoop. "This is *kicked to the curb*."

"Can we sue?"

"Interesting little bit of trivia. When they promoted me to management—if you call it that—a year ago, I signed a non-litigation clause. We can't sue."

Their exchange of "But couldn't we?" and "No, and here's why" consumed the next few minutes and continued when they took the discussion into the house. They swapped sides—Trey introducing ideas and Vicki felling them with reality.

Someone in corporate made a decision, circling Trey's name as an "expendable." Just shy of retirement? All the better.

Did the soulless creature handing out pink slips have any idea how the fingernails of disaster would scrape against the exposed skin of those affected?

If that person wasn't soulless, how did he or she live with himself or herself?

No matter how bad the business, moral, or ethical decision, Trey and Vicki—and thousands like them—are left with the endless, unfading echo: "Now what? What do we do now?"

Retelling the story reaches a point where it brings no improvement, only further disintegration of trust, reputations, and our ability to cope. We can rehearse the injustice of it all until we're hoarse. Or we can regroup with tough choices we shouldn't have to make, revisions we didn't dream we'd need, plans that bear no resemblance to the ones we've entertained since signing up for a Social Security number.

The phrase *game changer* appears on lists of clichés these days. People like Trey and Vicki would add *dream changer* to the list.

Their savings hadn't ever gotten a good start. Friends in similar circumstances were worse off than they were. One couple cosigned their son's student loans for graduate school. When the son defaulted, unable to pay, the debt fell to the parents, who found their dinner table conversations punctuated with a word they'd thought would never cross their lips in this context—bankruptcy.

Trey reached for an antacid one day and stopped mid-reach. The excess bile in his stomach wasn't because of their circumstances, but because of indignation against those who'd caused their circumstances. The negative impact of a precarious situation was intensified by Trey's tenacious hold on his right to be angry about its injustice.

The anger of man, the Bible tells us, does not accomplish the purposes of God (James 1:20).

Trey's fuming didn't change anything for the better. It hadn't made his former employer listen to reason. It hadn't altered their financial picture. It rotted his stomach, soured the air in their home, and weakened his ability to move forward.

So he gave up the habit. Cold turkey. With a handful of relapses.

He's working again. On the sanity maintenance crew—maintaining a positive attitude and strengthening his core. Like most survival moves, it began with a decision to do something different than what wasn't working.

Trey and Vicki are so not alone. The details may be different, but young people looking to start a family are finding it impossible to secure a job with benefits. Too many companies are making do with part-time employees to cut their costs of operation. Employees approaching retirement age no longer gloat that they're "almost there," because they've heard stories of others whose retirements were aborted. Men and women working long hours still can't manage their mortgage payments.

It doesn't seem remotely fair.

Corporate decisions like the one that affected Trey aren't uncommon. Some of those decisions sicken the bosses forced to make the calls.

Nobody likes the situation.

A few have mastered the art of survival, although they would label *mastered* too strong a word.

"We're simplifying our lives," one couple reports, "and in many ways it's freeing."

"We tossed pride aside and took jobs we thought we wouldn't appreciate but discovered unexpected joys, like the people we've met and skills we didn't know we had."

"It's hard. I won't deny that. We have our low moments—drainage ditch low. But we're getting a better grip on what really matters in life."

Is it a futile exercise to grab for mere scraps of hope when faced with devastating news?

Is it futile to latch onto something floating in the water after a boat capsizes? No. It's a saving grace.

———

Reflections:

1. "The LORD loves justice," reads Psalm 37:28. His overarching plans include restoring justice where it's been absent. In situations like the one Trey and Vicki faced, confidence in God's sense of justice was a holding-on place in the cliff they scaled. When has it meant the most to you?

2. How could pride get in the way of answers for Trey and Vicki?

3. When have you had to delete a long-held dream and sketch out another to take its place? What helped equip you to think creatively about workable solutions?

If you know a *Trey* . . .

You no doubt do. When researching this chapter, I heard the same story with minor variations from every corner. Financial injustice? The pool of pain is wide and deep. And everyone's in the pool.

How do you walk that fine line between showing excess sympathy, which can be demeaning and disheartening, and acting "too" normal around a couple faced with financial devastation?

"Just ask," God says. "You need to know what to say, how to act? You lack wisdom? Just ask." James 1:5 tells us, "Anyone who needs wisdom should ask God, whose very nature is to give to everyone without a second thought, without keeping score. Wisdom will certainly be given to those who ask."

———

God's handiwork is honesty and justice;
all God's rules are trustworthy—
they are established always and forever.
PSALM 111:7-8

22. 'Til Death Do Us In

Tasha

CHANGING DOCTORS FELT LIKE MOVING CROSS-country and demanded at least as much fortitude, Tasha thought. "Let's just relive the pain as many times as we can." She sighed as she sat in an unfamiliar exam room, with a stranger's name on the diplomas on the wall.

The new medical assistant had handled the endless list of questions admirably when taking Tasha's vitals and recording yet another version of her medical history. The girl hadn't flinched at the term *AIDS*. Bless her.

For most of her life, left to wait in a paper gown on a paper-draped exam table, Tasha would have swung her legs to keep her feet from getting cold. She no longer had the energy.

The bones in her wrists ached. The pain *du jour*. Her skin breakdown was a concern she'd have to discuss with Dr.—she glanced at the diploma—Sterling. Kathryn Sterling.

The door opened to admit Dr. Sterling. She must have been one of those who entered medical school as a preteen. Sleek chestnut hair cascaded in a loose braid over her shoulder. It reached almost to her perfectly formed baby bump.

Tasha had chopped her long hair short after her last hospitalization. Easier to take care of. She'd never had a baby bump to work around.

Nice to meet you.

Nice to meet you, too.

"So," the good doctor continued, adjusting her stethoscope necklace, "AIDS, huh?"

"Anniversary gift from my husband."

The doctor's eyes widened. The pronouncement always had that effect.

Dr. Sterling listened, looked, adjusted medications, suggested a nutritional supplement, and wrote a name on a slip of paper.

"What's this?" Tasha held the paper gown closed in front of her as she read the name.

"A friend of mine who counsels people entering late-stage AIDS. She specializes in cases like yours."

Tasha laid the note in her lap and rubbed her aching wrist. "Cases like mine? Where my death sentence came from someone I love?"

Every medical appointment dragged her thoughts back to the first one—the one when she heard the you-must-be-mistaken diagnosis. Her brow hadn't uncreased yet. It had been six years.

She'd gone home that day and changed clothes for the second anniversary dinner her always-the-romantic husband had planned at a restaurant several stars up from their normal fare. They'd made it to dessert before he asked, "Hey, how'd your appointment go?"

She knew her own history. Parts of his were still a mystery. "Collin, did you ever have a blood transfusion?"

His spoon bit through the crust of his crème brulee. "No."

"During college, you spent some time in Africa, right?"

"Yes. Are you dodging the real issue, Tasha? I asked how your appointment went."

She stared into the candle flame, afraid of what she'd see in his eyes. "Did you work at an AIDS station there?"

"No, construction. Why the—?" His spoon stilled.

Tasha raised her gaze to look full in the face of the man she'd vowed to love and cherish, the man she'd saved herself for, the man she believed had saved himself for her. "Then you need to be tested. You need to start talking about what you haven't told me. I'm HIV-positive and you have some explaining to do."

He was sorry, so sorry. That helped. Not enough to change the outcome, but enough to give her a handhold while they waited. He prayed she'd be one for whom nothing further would develop. She wasn't.

He cursed God. That intensified her pain. It . . . wasn't . . . God's . . . fault.

God was responsible for her ability to keep loving the one whose sins nailed her to a hospital bed, the one whose past meant she'd never be a mother, the one who was sorry but inept at rising above his guilt to address the real problem.

"I get it now," she said. "I understand a little of the extravagance of Jesus. Knowing what they'd done, He made a decision to keep loving people who caused His pain, undeserved pain, friends who wrote His death sentence."

She breathed in through invisible but choking dusty-gray ash. "Since the day I first heard His story, I've been grateful for what He did. Through all this"—she gestured to the parade of medications at her elbow, the angry-looking IV site in her forearm, the shadow her body had become—"I've gained a far greater respect and reverence for what it cost Jesus to keep loving us."

Collin left her. It was too distressing to watch her suffer.

The morning he deserted her, she heard a rooster crow.

People experiencing intense heartache often report a heightened sensitivity to what some call the whispers of God. Though not audible, the hurting ones sense conversations between their mental self and their soul self, as David the psalmist did.

Why, I ask myself, are you so depressed?
Why are you so upset inside?
    Hope in God!
    Because I will again give him thanks,
    my saving presence and my God. (Psalm 42:11)

Tasha carried on conversations between her soul self and the God she clung to when all was stripped away.

"Just let me be angry for a while, God!"

"Okay."

"*Okay?*"

"I understand why you'd want to claw his eyes out."

"But You won't let me do that?"

"A rhetorical question, right?"

Tasha and the still, small, universe-rattling Voice continued their discussion.

"It's completely unfair that I should have to bear this when Collin is the one who messed up!"

"No argument there."

"So, You'll help me?"

"Help you maintain your anger? No."

"But . . ."

"It's costing you energy you need for fighting this disease. Work with Me here."

Tasha's faith convinced her that even if God didn't use those specific words, He held that specific intention for her and cared intimately enough to serve as moment-by-moment Guide through the muck of her husband's choices.

It's often been said that if we each threw our distresses into a big pile in the middle of the room and were given the opportunity to choose someone else's pain, we'd think for a moment, then reach for the one that was already ours.

We don't like the one we came into the room with. But we wouldn't want someone else's either.

The intensity of Tasha's circumstances steals the breath of even casual onlookers. And we're helpless to make a difference for her. We can't remove the disease or its devastation. We can't make her husband "man up" and help shoulder the burden he inflicted on her. We can't find words that soothe. As much as we wish we could, we can't fully understand what she's going through on any level.

And if you do identify all too closely with the fallout ash through which Tasha is crawling . . .

May God's peace envelop you. Nothing else is strong enough.

Reflections:

1. Horrified. Mortified. Devastated. And those were only the emotional effects of the disease and the prognosis Tasha bore, undeserved. The physical effects needed words that haven't been invented yet. Sharing common ground with Jesus poured a coating of holiness over her distress. Still horrible, but unspeakably profound. In what ways do your distresses parallel that kind of suffering? In what ways do Tasha's far outdistance yours?

2. How natural is it for you to feel the need to explain, "It

wasn't my fault!" when others observe the consequences you're bearing for someone else's choices? Imagine how exhausting it must be for Tasha and others like her to rehearse the story. Without discounting the role the other person played or making excuses for his or her behavior, is there a way we can relate enough of the story to be real without sharing more information than necessary or information that makes us feel vindicated but in the process vilifies someone else in need of grace?

3. Do you wrestle with Tasha's statement that it "wasn't . . . God's . . . fault"? What do you know about the character of God that supports her conviction and yours?

If you know a *Tasha* . . .

There are no words.

All that remains is unconditional, extravagant love.

—

But I will rejoice in the LORD;
I will celebrate his salvation.
*All my bones will say, "*LORD, *who could compare to you?*
You rescue the weak from those who overpower them;
you rescue the weak and the needy from
those who plunder them."

PSALM 35:9-10

23. Tug of Family War

Jolee

KIM CAPPED THE DRY-ERASE MARKER AND SET IT in the aluminum tray at the base of the board. "Does that make sense, students? I'm looking for these three things in your artwork today. Color. Movement, as we discussed earlier. And storytelling. I want to be able to 'read' your picture as if it were a story without words. Do your best work. The festival art committee will choose six pictures from each classroom for the gallery wall display. You'll have a half hour today. Then we'll take time tomorrow to complete your projects, if you want to add anything. Go ahead and begin."

Her first graders tore into the project with high energy. All except Jolee. Jolee's window-staring, which Kim had assumed equivalent to waiting for inspiration, turned catatonic.

"Having a hard time getting started, Jolee?"

The girl's hair hung in her face when she dropped her gaze to the blank paper on the desk in front of her.

"Do you need an idea?"

Hair swung from side to side.

"Any aspect of the holidays, Jolee. Whatever you'd like."

Still no response.

"How about making a picture of your family at the Thanksgiving meal? Or watching football together. Decorating the tree? No? Opening gifts? Do you go caroling together or play games?"

"I hate the holidays."

"We don't like to use that word in our classroom, Jolee. Make another choice."

Her swath of palomino hair secured behind her ear, the little girl said, "I hate Thanksgiving. I hate Christmas. I hate my birthday." She snatched a black crayon from the pile and dug a storm of lines across the page.

Kim squatted beside the desk, positioning herself at eye level with her student. She laid her hand across Jolee's white knuckles and stilled the artless fury. "Do you want to tell me what's going on?"

Kim didn't need to hear the words. She could guess. Not at all confident the girl would expose her heart with a classroom of oblivious amateur artists buzzing around them, Kim held her breath when the hurting one began to speak.

"What does my family do at the holidays?" Her tone disturbingly matter-of-fact, Jolee said, "They fight. That's what they do. They fight over me."

"Are your parents divorced?"

"Yes, but I get that. I mean, I get it that people divorce. I don't get why they have to take it out on me."

The last words faded. Kim leaned closer, but Jolee offered no further explanation. "Do they . . . hurt you?"

Jolee shot her a crooked look. "Well, *yeah*-uh."

"Hit you?"

"No. Not that way."

Kim glanced at the roomful of students. "Can we talk about this after class?"

"I guess."

"Sometimes it helps to have someone listen."

Kim listened to yet another in a long list of heartbreaking stories affecting her students. This time, a couple found a way to end their marriage but not their vindictiveness, which they spread liberally, particularly generous with it at the holidays and special occasions. They fought over who got Jolee for Christmas Eve versus Christmas morning, who had her for Thanksgiving Day and who had to move the celebration to the weekend, how much was too much to spend on a six-year-old, and who made the other one more miserable.

"I'm Mary in the Sunday school pageant this year," she said. "I hope neither one of them comes to see it. They'll mess everything up."

"How?"

"They'll look at each other like this." Jolee scrunched her mouth and glared, arms crossed.

"I'm so sorry."

"Sometimes I think I'm more grown up than they are."

Kim projected ahead to a future hostility-laced wedding with the Hatfields and the McCoys refusing to lay down their verbal weapons for the sake of Jolee's happiness. She envisioned Jolee as a parent, watching the grandparents play tug-of-war with another generation of children.

The hug Kim gave Jolee that afternoon held an unspoken message.

Little one, I've been there. It doesn't get easier.

Divorce happens. We wish it didn't. Can children survive the divorce of their parents? Sure. Can they survive unscathed, untouched, unmarred?

Wistfulness creeps into the tone of voice when a child of divorce—even a forty- or fifty-year-old "child"—talks about when his or her parents split up. That disappointment takes on a far darker, stain-like tone when the parents made or still make life unbearable for everyone around them postdivorce.

How would Jolee describe it at forty? "You've wrecked the holidays for me. You've ruined the idea of summer vacation. The thought of my birthday party makes me tense, not because of how old I am, but because of the fuss it turns into when you keep the war alive."

It's hard for a child of divorce to say, "Not my problem. Your gripes against one another are not my responsibility." It's true, but also true is the cloud of fallout that drifts onto the children of divorce.

As she matures, Jolee may find ways to negotiate with her parents and stepparents. Maneuvering the minefield of their hostility will likely prove treacherous. But she may succeed in laying out a truce plan for sharing holidays, birthdays, special occasions, and, with the help of a wise counselor, talking through a set of ground rules for the family members' ongoing interpersonal relationships.

Will conflicts magically disappear? No.

Jolee may never be free of what it feels like to have a parent tugging on each arm.

So where's the hope for her and all the others like her?

"Don't let it get to you, honey."

"Quit caring what your parents think. Do what's right for you."

"The moon'll come out . . . tomorrow."

Not much comfort there.

Why is this book titled *Ragged Hope?* Why doesn't it have a crisper title like *Fresh-Pressed Hope: Smoothing Your Way Through Other People's Choices?*

Because hope takes a beating. Its edges show wear from the tugging of heartbreaks like divorce. But a hope breathed into existence by God boasts integrity that endures despite raw edges. And that's what makes it worth clinging to in crises.

The spittle of parental hostility always lands on the children. A feud between Mom and Dad is as hard to breathe through as secondhand smoke.

Jolee has a caring teacher willing to listen, who understands what it feels like to be the collateral damage in divorce. Will her parents find a more amicable way of working out their differences, minimizing the aftershocks for their child? Maybe. I pray they do.

And if not? I pray Jolee keeps clinging to her ragged-edged hope and that she always has someone like Kim nearby. I pray I'll be sensitive to know when it's my turn to be Kim.

———

Reflections:

1. Think hard. Have your vindictive words about another person—a coworker, spouse, former spouse, church member—poisoned someone else's opinion, or fouled the air at work, at home, at church? Is making someone else

wretchedly unhappy worth the temporary relief of voicing your own distress?

2. If you're divorced, have you found an amicable way of relating to one another? Would your children consider your attitude mature despite your hurt or disappointment?

3. If you're a child of divorce, what have you done to keep the fallout to a minimum? How do you deal with recurring waves of disappointment and tension? Do you have a trusted friend you can lean on, someone who listens well—both to you and to God—who dishes out advice sparingly and sensitively but doesn't shy away from truth-telling? Someone who feeds your courage? Have you made finding that person a matter of prayer?

If you know a *Jolee* . . .

Jolee lost her parents, her sense of home, and then watched her mom and dad destroy the joy-producers—the events and activities a child would normally look forward to, if not for the fighting.

You have within you the ability to infuse joy into sometimes joyless situations for young people like Jolee. Who in your circle of influence needs to hear, "I'm willing to listen if you'd like to talk"?

Only God is my rock and my salvation—my stronghold!—
I won't be shaken anymore.

PSALM 62:2

24. Dangerous Obsession

Jenni

HER BONES SHOOK, JOINTS RATTLING LIKE A SCIENCE class skeleton. Willow ended the call and pressed the phone to her chest. "God, please protect them!"

The rest of her prayer sounded more like a groan than a sentence.

How many more threats would Gary make against her sister and their children before someone intervened? Gary's intimidation tactics worked well. He still controlled them all, despite the divorce, despite the restraining order, despite the court decisions.

Always one step shy of crossing a serious legal line, his hot breath of intimidation scorched them. They felt watched, stalked, as if waiting for a sniper bullet. It didn't take much imagination to move that bullet from a rhetorical device, a metaphorical word picture of his twisted anger, to a genuine possibility.

Jenni and Willow both heard their mother's counsel echoing through time. "Watch out for the jealous ones. They're dangerous."

Neither sister remembered an addendum: "And they'll ruin your life."

But here it was, the fallout of an ex-husband's misdirected, pathological, illogical, and unfounded jealous rage. After a quiet six months, with Gary's attentions apparently directed elsewhere, their tentative peace was shattered with a peppering of phone calls that rekindled the fires of fear.

Jenni thought he'd moved on. She prayed he'd moved on. But she couldn't pray he'd find someone else. It wouldn't be fair to the someone else.

Willow poured herself a cup of coffee and didn't wait for it to cool. It scalded her throat on the way down. She didn't waste energy cringing when she needed every bit of it for supporting her sister and kids in their impossible situation. Willow couldn't invite them to live with her. Gary knew her neighborhood almost as well as he did theirs. She'd suggested two reputable women's shelters, one of which Jenni had taken advantage of before the divorce. But the shelters were temporary.

And the piece of paper that dissolved their marriage had no effect on the man's pulsing, insane rage.

Jenni's church family saw no hint of Gary's dark side. A skilled con artist, he flipped a switch on Sunday mornings and pulled off the ruse with Oscar-worthy perfection. Jenni was the one ostracized when she filed for divorce. The church rallied behind Gary. How could she? How could she leave such a fine, godly man and rob him of the opportunity to be with his children? How could she make up those evil stories about him?

They'd never seen a bruise or scar and never seen anything but the joy of Jesus on his face. His "thriving marriage" Sunday school sessions were among the most requested. His voice rose above the congregation in worship. His prayers for others were heartfelt and sensitive, his empathetic tears heart-melting.

What was her problem?

The fact that the courts awarded her full custody didn't sway public opinion. So Jenni and the children lost their church in the divorce, too. And now, with Gary's threats and intimidation escalating again, Jenni saw no recourse but to move to another part of the country.

Willow stiffened at the thought. "It's hard to disappear these days," she'd said on the phone. "Hard to relocate to a place where a rabid man can't find you with a few clicks of a computer." She knew her sister wasn't unaware of that fact. But someone had to say it aloud.

And Jenni shouldn't have to move. She shouldn't be the one to pay the price for his insanity. She'd already been drained of so much.

Willow's life had changed, too. Concern remained on this side of worry only because of the effort she expended to keep it that way. She'd left a promising job to move closer to her sister and help however she could. Her new job stunk by comparison, but seemed a small price to pay considering the distress that ruled Jenni's life. If Jenni and the kids disappeared, would she go with them?

That wasn't a decision she could make on her own. She opened her Bible. Black ink on thin pages. "Lord . . ."

Nothing more came.

She turned on the television, then switched it off. The news reported another domestic dispute that ended tragically. Across town. Not Jenni's address. Wrong number of kids. Wrong description. But too close.

She added another row of cement blocks to the hedge of protection she prayed around Jenni and the little ones. When she opened her Bible again, this time the page in front of her read,

> The salvation of the righteous
>> comes from the LORD;
>>> he is their refuge in times of trouble.
> The LORD will help them

and rescue them—
rescue them from the wicked—
and he will save them
because they have taken refuge in him.
(Psalm 37:39-40)

Willow flipped a few pages and read,

You hide them
in the shelter of your wings,
safe from human scheming.
You conceal them in a shelter,
safe from accusing tongues.
(Psalm 31:20)

If *amen* means "let it be so," Willow thought, then her string of a thousand amens seemed more than appropriate.

If heaven kept a log of categories, prayers for protection for loved ones would likely tower over other requests on the bar graph. My friend Willow's concern for her sister's safety from her ex-husband's rages would be well represented on that graph. The fallout of fear blankets daily life, constricting them, dumping a pall on the simplest activity, like grocery shopping. Will he show up? What will he do? Will he try to take the kids, hurt them or her? If his threats are to be believed, their fears aren't unfounded.

What hope can survive that kind of oppression?

Willow and her sister point to Hebrews 6:18-19, verses that have taken on new meaning in light of their trauma. "[God] did this [pledged the promise of his purposes] so that we, who have taken refuge in him, can be encouraged to grasp the hope that is lying in front of us. This hope . . . is a safe and secure anchor for our whole being."

Hope. In front of us for the taking.

Hope. Lying on top of a pile of hopelessness. Only God could do that.

Why didn't this story include a happily-ever-after ending? Because in this life, stories don't always end that way. And Jenni's story is ongoing. Willow and her sister are in the middle of an unabridged dictionary-thick drama. Other books and professional counselors can give advice on how to bring the story to a conclusion, when it's possible. This book is devoted to ragged hope—to surviving until rescue arrives.

A pat answer—a sappy quip like "Hang in there"— is not only offensive but borders on ridiculous when the stakes are so high. But we have to have holding-on places, those razor-narrow footholds on the cliff face, the fingertip-deep shelves of rock to which we can cling.

Reflections:

1. What are your footholds and handholds? When fear threatens, what do you reach out to grip? How do you catch your breath?
2. A woman caught in a situation similar to Jenni's says that even in the worst times, she forces herself to do something

joy-producing for fifteen minutes. Her brain, heart, and nerves need the breather. With the drama raging around her, she retreats to a fifteen-minute pocket of something that refreshes her soul—a book, a hot bath, a quick walk through an art gallery, a cup of tea on the front porch. Her husband's control issues dictate too much already. She wrestles back fifteen minutes of peace, which feeds her reserves to keep pressing on. What would your fifteen minutes look like?

3. Jenni can't afford to focus on the idea that life should be fair. She can't exhaust herself screaming for justice or she'll have nothing left with which to move forward, no strength to devote to protecting her young family and seeking God's answers to the question, "What now?" Is there a life circumstance in which you've been screaming, "No fair!" but have found it a futility exercise that accomplishes little and costs much? What approach have you found genuinely effective in unjust situations?

If you know a *Jenni* or a *Willow* . . .

Imagine how Jenni's load would lighten if she were believed, listened to, taken seriously. Drawing close to someone in that much pain isn't comfortable. And, like Willow, what we hear introduces our own battles with fear. But we can't escape God's instructions for us to "carry each other's burdens and so . . . fulfill the law of Christ"(Galatians 6:2).

When a young elephant is weakened by a traumatic

experience, the stronger elephants form a circle around the injured one—whether it was his own fault or not—to create a safe place for the young elephant to catch its breath and heal. The circle is a threat to threats. Its formidable wall of protection keeps predators at bay and gives time for the vulnerable one to regain his strength to fight for himself.

Do you serve as part of a circle like that for a vulnerable friend or family member? Please don't underestimate the simple act of being there. Your quiet presence is a powerful threat to threats. As has been true through the centuries, God magnifies the imposing nature of a circle of caring friends to thwart ambushes and send enemies running.

Father of orphans and defender of widows
is God in his holy habitation.
PSALM 68:5

The wicked draw their swords and bend their bows
to bring down the weak and the needy,
to slaughter those whose way is right.
But the sword of the wicked will enter their own hearts!
Their bows will be broken!
PSALM 37:14-15

25. Anyway

Zeke

AS WE WAITED IN THE CORRIDOR OUTSIDE THE courtroom—not our typical destination on a random Thursday afternoon—we overheard Zeke's lawyer tell him, "Let me do the talking. Don't say anything more than 'Yes, sir' or 'No, sir' unless he asks you a direct question."

"I know the routine," Zeke said, an obvious edge of impatience in his voice. He rubbed off the rough spots and added, "Thanks."

Eight of us crowded into the narrow hallway of the local

courthouse. Zeke tugged at his wholly uncustomary necktie. He wasn't the only one out of his element. Most of us hadn't been inside a courtroom. We'd seen plenty of them on the news and in television dramas. But other than minor traffic violations for which we'd promptly paid our fines or when applying for a passport, we'd had no reason to enter the courthouse building, much less one of the courtrooms. We'd never locked eyes, or avoided eye contact, with a judge.

We were there that day because of Zeke. We volunteered to serve as character witnesses for a changed life.

As one, we prayed for favor for our friend, a young man once trapped by a string of incredibly lousy choices, now putting as much distance as possible between his past and his hope-threaded future. But he had one more court date. One more offense to answer for. One more sentencing for one more sin.

Would our voices be considered? Would the judge listen to a motley crew of middle-aged churchgoers who viewed the tattooed, pierced, braided accused as our brother in Christ?

We weren't as naïve as we might have appeared. We knew Zeke's ongoing struggles. Most of them. We knew better than to assume he'd never again be tempted to break the law. But we also knew he operated, as he tells it, "under a new influence—the power of Jesus Christ," to whom he'd waved a white flag in a heaven-stirring dance of surrender.

The double doors of Courtroom Three opened and admitted Zeke, his lawyer, and us, Zeke's entourage of friends.

The representative from the district attorney's office joined Zeke and his lawyer as they approached the bench. We filed into the two rows of seats on the right. I couldn't help thinking, "friends of the bride or friends of the groom?"

I briefly wondered how long it had been since that many Jesus followers occupied chairs in this courtroom. My wandering thoughts were interrupted by the words, "All rise."

We knew the current offense warranted jail time. We also knew that for Zeke to head back into that atmosphere at this stage of his newly kindled faith would risk a setback. Willing to pay the penalty he owed, even if that meant more jail time and another delay to his stepping into a future marked by both internal and external freedom, Zeke faced the judge.

The defense attorney's plans to "do all the talking" were thwarted by the judge's determination to address Zeke directly. "Who are all these people?" he asked.

Zeke stuck his hands in his pants pockets. His lawyer nudged him with her elbow. He withdrew his hands and gestured toward us. "They're my friends, Your Honor." Then he introduced us all by name.

The judge's eyebrows rose. "And they're here to . . . ?"

Zeke looked at his lawyer, who nodded. "They're here to show me their support, Your Honor."

"They're the ones who wrote these character reference letters, Zeke?"

"Yes, sir."

"I've read them all. It appears you're hanging with a different caliber of friends these days."

"Yes."

"What?"

"Yes, sir, Your Honor."

The judge shifted in his high-backed chair, tapped the papers in front of him with the blunt end of his pen, then laid it down and clamped his hands together, resting them on the court documents that delineated the charges against Zeke.

"The letters all say you're a changed man."

"Yes, sir. I am."

"Lots of people say that when they stand in front of me."

"I understand that, sir. I have a whole new set of values."

The judge lifted his two-handed fist then set it back down. "That's what your friends tell me."

How long would this drag on? Others in the chairs next to me squirmed, letting me know I wasn't alone in wishing it was over. Jail or no jail? We'll deal with either.

"Zeke, tell these friends of yours more of your story."

The look on the judge's face might have been a smirk, but I didn't want to believe that.

"Is this your first offense?"

"No, Your Honor."

"Of what other crimes have you been convicted?"

Zeke swallowed so loud we heard it in the back of the room. "All of them?"

"I have time if you do. Tell these friends what you've done."

Was that ethical? Legal? Neither Zeke's lawyer or the district attorney's rep objected.

So the list began.

In discussing the bizarre forced confessional later that day, we observers remarked about our similar thought patterns. As Zeke rattled off what he'd done, what made him a frequent visitor to courtrooms like that, to a person we were thinking, "We know. And we love him anyway."

"Your Honor, I was convicted of . . ."

We know. We love you anyway.

"I served time for . . ."

We know. We love you anyway.

"And I . . . "

We know. We love you anyway.

Why? Because Jesus does.

As the minutes and the offenses ticked by, we formed predictions about how much time Zeke would be asked to serve. When he stopped talking, the judge nodded, sighed, and said, "The kind of mercy the court can show and the kind of mercy God shows are two different things, young man."

All eight of us observers sat up a little straighter.

"But I see the change in you."

Yes! We do, too!

"And I believe I can take into consideration the assessment of your new friends."

Yes!

"Your parents are here in the courtroom today, Zeke?"

"Yes, sir."

"They've known you a long time."

"Since the day I was born, sir."

A smile broke the flat plain of the judge's face. "I imagine they're pleased with the changes they've seen in you."

In that nanosecond of time, I imagined the kind of fallout his parents bore watching their son spend his youth self-destructing . . . and the peace they now tentatively embraced.

"I'm pleased, too," the judge affirmed. "From what I've observed and read, I believe the change in you is genuine. Two years probation."

And a monetary fine, to which neither lawyer objected.

"I've seen you in my courtroom many times over the years, Zeke."

"Yes, sir."

"The next time we cross paths, let's pray we have something else to talk about. Fishing, perhaps."

Zeke smiled and turned toward us, then back toward the judge. "Yes, sir. Fishing."

The Zeke we're still watching grow is building a repertoire of positive decisions, one at a time. His steps were halting, stuttering at first. Frustration brought him to the edge of what could have threatened to pull him back toward danger. We who love him applauded wildly every time he made a smart, healing, mature, God-honoring decision. In the process, we caught a fresh glimpse of how heaven must applaud when each of us makes smart decisions for our own lives.

It might have seemed the "fallout of other people's choices" part of Zeke's story occupied little space—the brief mention of the impact of Zeke's bad choices on his caring parents. A lifetime of mourning.

But another layer of "fallout" spreads itself throughout these few pages.

When Zeke made a decision to abandon his old lifestyle for new life, that choice affected an ever-widening circle of people whose faith grew as they watched his fledgling faith take off. His unquenchable appetite for God's radiant Word reminded us what a wonder we held in our hands. His appreciation of grace magnified our own.

A life redeemed will do that.

Reflections:

1. Parents often wait years beyond what they think is their hearts' limit to see results of intense prayer for their child. We're bound by the constraints of time, frustrated when God's methods don't match our own designs, fearful that the answers will never come. If you've long waited for answers to prayer for your child, how did you manage the waiting time?

2. Has someone prayed long and hard for you? Over what issue? Is the concern for you founded, legitimate? How do you explain your resistance to allowing that person to see her or his prayers answered?

3. Are you the same person you were in your teens? How have you changed? What have you done to shake off the reputation created by the person you once were?

If you know a *Zeke* . . .

Consider him a gift to your faith. Yes, he may make you nervous, challenge you to walk through doors you never imagined, keep you on your knees. But he may also ignite a new fire in your faith and open your eyes to graces you've taken for granted.

———

Christ has set us free for freedom. Therefore stand firm and don't submit to the bondage of slavery again.

GALATIANS 5:1

26. Watermark

Cynthia

MY OWN STORY IS WOVEN INTO THE FABRIC OF the others in this book. The people you read about in the previous pages are real people I know—some family members and close friends, others people whose paths I've crossed in thirty-three years of leading retreats and hosting *The Heartbeat of the Home* radio broadcast. Their names and unessential details have been fictionalized for the sake of their privacy and their continued healing.

Their stories moved me because I identified with a flash of

this, a thread of that. In some cases, I grieved as if a friend's tragedy had happened to me. In some cases, the tragedy *had* happened to me. In others, I listened, sympathized, then raced home, breathing hard and thanking the Lord that their path was not mine.

I took a break from writing to watch a television documentary. Moments after it started, I realized I was watching this book. The program documented some of the thousands of stories tied to the moment in history marked by a date recognized around the world—September 11.

I found myself holding my breath, as I had the day it happened, still disbelieving after all these years. Footage of firefighters and police officers running into harm's way constricted my throat. I could almost feel the heat from the fires—jet fuel, offices, and bodies ablaze. Agony etched on the faces of eyewitnesses took me back to the moment when I watched the sickening drama unfold live, leaning on my kitchen counter near the small TV screen with my hand pressed to my racing heart.

From every angle, cameras caught the horrifying scene as the first tower came down. Then the second.

Who of us doesn't hold onto the images of the cloud of ash, concrete dust, and shattered glass racing like a formless monster through the streets?

When the dust settled, it lay like a blanket of nuclear fallout over the broken scene.

Too few survivors stumbled through the ash cloud, stunned, surprised they were alive.

My heart constricted when in the process of writing this book I keyed in the choices people made that created nuclear-like destruction for others. Like the tokens of life at Ground Zero—a survivor unearthed, the story of someone who missed being among the lost because his alarm didn't go off that morning, an American flag planted in the rubble—hope, however tattered, rose from these pages. I saw hope as a watermark between the lines, superimposed over every heartache.

While recording these *Ragged Hope* stories, I pored over the Bible, knowing only God holds a breath of hope for people living in the aftermath of other people's choices. My search led me to a passage with which I thought I was familiar—Psalm 107. Maybe like me, you'll reexamine what it says and how it applies to those living in the fallout of consequences.

"Let the redeemed of the LORD say so," reads Psalm 107:2 (NASB). One translation words it this way: "Let the redeemed of the LORD *tell their story*" (TNIV, emphasis mine).

From there, the psalmist describes four groups of "the redeemed," how they found themselves in trouble, what they did about it, how God responded, and what God expected in return.

Some had wandered (verse 4); some had been sitting in darkness and gloom, imprisoned because they disobeyed God's instructions (verses 10-11); some were fools because of their bad choices (verse 17); and some were innocently minding their own business, in the midst of worshiping God's wonders (verse 24).

In each case, what did they do about it, according to this passage? They "cried out to the LORD in their distress" (verses 6, 13, 19, 28).

How did God respond? "God delivered them from their desperate circumstances" (verses 6, 13, 19, 28).

Note that this particular translation, the Common English Bible, lists three angles to that response. Verse 6—"God delivered them." Verses 13 and 19—"God saved them." Verse 28—"God brought them out safe."

What did the Lord expect in return? "Let them thank the LORD for his faithful love and his wondrous works for all people" (verses 8, 15, 21, 31).

It didn't matter who or what was the source of distress— their own foolishness, the cruelty of others, disobedience, or just the pummeling waves of life—the pattern remained (and still remains) the same.

We cry out to the Lord in our distress.

He delivers us from our desperate circumstances.

And we in turn thank the Lord for His faithful love and His wondrous works for all people.

It doesn't matter if it was my fault or someone else's bad decision. The protocol is the same. Cry out to God. Watch God work on my behalf. Express my gratitude.

Did you catch the heart-soothing poetry within that passage?

The [people's] courage melted at this terrible situation . . .
[but] *God quieted* the storm to a whisper;
  the sea's waves were hushed.
So they rejoiced because the waves
  had calmed down;
  then *God led them to the harbor they were hoping for*
(Psalm 107: 26, 29-30, emphasis mine).

The harbor they were hoping for.

Did you notice the hope-laced sentence tucked into verse 41? "But God raises the needy from their suffering."

There they are—caught in the backwash, the aftermath, the fallout of other people's choices, suffering because of decisions others made that changed their lives into grueling exercises in endurance or tainted what should be sweet memories with the emotional equivalent of acid rain.

But God.

But God raises them up out of it.

Hope isn't always glitzy and sparkly. Sometimes it looks worn around the edges. But it's irrepressible, durable, and essential for those who live in the shadow of bad decisions others make.

We cling to a hope that gets knocked around and trampled on. Do we still call it hope? Is it cross-your-fingers wishing things would change? Or is it deeper, bigger, more enduring than that? More durable—"able to exist for a long time without significant deterioration" (*Merriam Webster*, www.merriam-webster.com).

One can also think of *hope* as "eager anticipation." Of what? That the pain will go away? That the problem or person will go away? That our wrenching memories won't matter anymore? It has to be more than that.

It's an expectation based on the belief that God cares and that He can reach through the fallout to redeem, revive, refresh, restore.

A recent Barna survey proposed that as many as 70 percent of us feel held back by our pasts. Seventy percent, stuck in the back eddies of regret—ours or others'—circling, circling, languishing.

Flooding the past with forgiveness is like raising the water level so the current takes us up and over rocks and partially submerged obstacles rather than our bashing against them. The rush of grace flushes us out of those back eddies and into the main branch of the river, where life teems.

Unforgiveness and resentment enslave us to the hurt, justified though they seem. When forced to bear the consequences of another's actions, we can't afford to be hamstrung by resentment.

But this isn't a how-to book. It isn't a how-come book. It's a celebration of the resiliency of the human spirit, the courageous resolve of those determined to survive despite the fallout of other people's choices, and the exquisite redemptive power of the God who can wring beauty from ashes.

Did you find your story within these chapters? Did you find your heart moved by stories vastly different from your own?

If you picked up this book because you are fighting hard to keep breathing through the ash cloud of someone else's choices, please know you are on my heart right now. I've held the thought of you tucked right here, above my pulse, through the writing of every word.

But of far greater importance is the assurance you are on God's heart. What did He do to get this book in your hands? Does it amaze you He would care enough to orchestrate those details?

If *Ragged Hope* accomplishes its purposes, it will help you breathe easier, feel understood, and send you running to Him.

We put our hope in the LORD.
He is our help and our shield.
Our heart rejoices in God because we trust his holy name.
LORD, *let your faithful love surround us,*
because we wait for you.

PSALM 33:20-22

Gratitude Journal

Lil Copan, editor and friend, thank you for turning a simple dinner conversation into an invitation to write this book. Our matched set of passions and compassions made working with you a profoundly enriching experience for me. My respect and gratitude for you and the Abingdon team is inexpressible in words, which is embarrassing for a writer to admit.

Lauren Winner, your eye for editing and your heart for the people for whom this book was written buoyed me as I honed and polished and prayed. Thank you for gracing this book with your attention and tender counsel.

Wendy Lawton, cherished agent but so much more, I leaned heavily on your encouragement and ocean-wide wisdom while committing these stories to paper. You cared so intensely about the people whom this book could reach that you inspired me to a greater depth of authenticity, digging even deeper for the choicest nuggets of hope.

The steady stream of prayers from Jackie, Becky, Elizabeth, my family, speaking audiences, the radio ministry support team, and our exceptional Life Group from North Ridge Church must have sounded like the cacophony of overlapped requests in the movie *Bruce Almighty*. It humbled me every time one of those dear friends told me they cared about this project and were praying as I wrote. It humbles me that they haven't deserted their posts.

Thank you, Bill, for holding me in your arms as you prayed for me.

I'm honored that Betsy A. Barber, PsyD., lent her time and expertise to affirm *Ragged Hope*'s message. Decades ago, we shared a dorm room. Still joined at the heart.

Beloved storytellers, you who rolled up your shirtsleeves so I could see your scars and write about them, may you be outrageously blessed for your courage. And may you thrive in the light of the Hope that glows in the dark.

And hope does not disappoint.
ROMANS 5:5 NASB

ABOUT THE AUTHOR

Cynthia Ruchti writes and produces the daily fifteen-minute radio broadcast, *The Heartbeat of the Home*, and is editor of the broadcast's *Backyard Friends* magazine. She served a two-year term as president of American Christian Fiction Writers and currently serves as ACFW's Professional Relations Liaison. In addition to writing novels, devotionals, and magazine articles, she speaks for women's events and writers' conferences. Cynthia and her plot-tweaking husband live in the heart of Wisconsin where she creates stories of Hope-that-glows-in-the-dark. Find Cynthia on the web at www.CynthiaRuchti.com.